Selected Poems

The Works of Carl Sandburg

POETRY

Billy Sunday and Other Poems
(edited by George and
Willene Hendrick)
Breathing Tokens (edited by
Margaret Sandburg)
Chicago Poems
*The Complete Poems of
Carl Sandburg*
Cornhuskers
Good Morning, America
Harvest Poems
Honey and Salt
The People, Yes
Slabs of the Sunburnt West
Smoke and Steel

NONFICTION

*Abraham Lincoln: The Prairie
Years* (two volumes)
*Abraham Lincoln: The Prairie
Years and the War Years*
(one-volume edition)
Abraham Lincoln: The War Years
(four volumes)
Always the Young Strangers
The American Songbag
The Chicago Race Riots

Home Front Memo
The Letters of Carl Sandburg
(edited by Herbert Mitgang)
Mary Lincoln: Wife and Widow
(documented by
Paul M. Angle)
Potato Face
The Sandburg Range
Steichen the Photographer
Storm over the Land

FICTION

Remembrance Rock

FOR CHILDREN

Abe Lincoln Grows Up
Arithmetic
Early Moon
More Rootabagas
Prairie-Town Boy
Rainbows Are Made
Rootabaga Pigeons
Rootabaga Stories
The Sandburg Treasury
*The Wedding Procession of the
Rag Doll and the Broom
Handle and Who Was in It*
Wind Song

❧ CARL SANDBURG

Selected Poems

Edited by George Hendrick
and Willene Hendrick

A HARVEST ORIGINAL
HARCOURT BRACE & COMPANY
San Diego   New York   London

Library of Congress Cataloging-in-Publication Data
Sandburg, Carl, 1878–1967.
    [Poems.   Selections]
    Selected poems/Carl Sandburg; edited by George Hendrick and
Willene Hendrick.
        p.   cm.
    "A Harvest original."
    Includes bibliographical references.
    ISBN 0-15-600396-1
    I. Hendrick, George.   II. Hendrick, Willene.
III. Title.
PS3537.A618A6   1996
811'.521—dc20   95-50686

Text set in Fournier
Designed by Kaelin Chappell
Printed in the United States of America
A Harvest Original
First edition 1996
F E D C B A

Contents

*Previously unpublished
†Posthumously published

Introduction

Carl Sandburg came to widespread public attention with the publication of his poem "Chicago" in Harriet Monroe's *Poetry* magazine in 1914. The opening lines are a vivid picture of the city as Sandburg saw it:

> Hog Butcher for the World,
> Tool Maker, Stacker of Wheat,
> Player with Railroads and the Nation's Freight Handler;
> Stormy, husky, brawling,
> City of the Big Shoulders.

The poem immediately "roused a storm of protest," one observer said. Many Chicagoans, as well as conservative readers everywhere, objected to Sandburg's brutal imagery, while other critics derided as unaesthetic his use of free verse. Nevertheless, two years later, when he published his first book-length volume, *Chicago Poems,* he used "Chicago" as the title poem. The poems in that book came from Sandburg's working-class background, his intimate knowledge of urban life based on his years as a journalist, his Socialist views, his belief in social and economic justice, and his faith in the people, "the mob."

Critical approaches to Sandburg's work were established early on. William Braithwaite, writing in the Boston *Transcript*, called *Chicago Poems* a "book of ill-regulated speech that has neither verse or proper rhythms." Amy Lowell objected to propagandistic elements in some of the poems but praised the originality of the book. W. A. Bradley, in the *Dial*, called Sandburg a "rather gross, simple-minded, sentimental" poet who was also a "highly sensitized impressionist who finds in the subtle accords between his own ideal moods and the loveliest, most elusive aspects of the external world, material for delicate and dreamlike expression."

Sandburg's early radicalism was tempered in the decades following the publication of *Chicago Poems*, and by the 1930s his poetry had lost some of its social sting. However, Sandburg himself never lost his social conscience or his Whitmanesque belief in the people, the American mob. After completing his six-volume biography of Lincoln in 1939, Sandburg became a cultural icon. He made appearances across the country reading his poetry and singing folk songs. While his racy and colloquial language never appealed to the academy, his poetry spoke to the masses and was accessible to all who could read. As Archibald MacLeish described it, "There is [in Sandburg's writing] . . . a tang, a liveliness, a pungency which is native and natural to the American ear."

Part of Sandburg's popularity can be attributed to his use of free verse. As he explained in *The Sandburg Treasury*:

> We have heard much in our time about free verse being modern, as though it is a new-found style for men to use in speaking and writing, rising out of the machine age, skyscrapers, high speed and jazz. Now, if free verse is a form of writing poetry without rhyme, without regular meters, without established and formal rules governing it, we can easily go back to the earliest styles of poetry known to the human family—and

the style is strictly free verse. Before men invented the alphabet, so that poems could be put down in writing, they spoke their poems. When one man spoke to another in a certain timebeat and rhythm, if it happened that his words conveyed certain impressions and moods to his listeners, he was delivering poetry to them, whether he knew it or they knew it, and whether he or they had a name for an art which the poet was practicing on himself and them.

This one-volume edition of Sandburg's best and most characteristic poetry is designed for general readers and for students. The poems span Sandburg's forty-year career and are drawn from four volumes: *The Complete Poems of Carl Sandburg,* published in 1970; *Breathing Tokens,* edited after Sandburg's death by his eldest daughter, Margaret Sandburg, in 1978; *Billy Sunday and Other Poems,* edited by George and Willene Hendrick in 1993; and *The World of Carl Sandburg,* by Norman Corwin, published in 1961. The poems are grouped by subject under eleven headings and are arranged within each section in roughly—though not slavishly— chronological order. Even if one wished to present the poems in strict chronological order, it would not be possible, for Sandburg rarely dated his poems. He tended to put them aside after they were written and would later dip into his kit bag to complete sections of whatever book he was preparing for publication at the time. At the end of this volume we list the original source of book publication of each poem in the anthology.

CHICAGO

Born to immigrant Swedish parents in the prairie town of Galesburg, Illinois, in 1876, Sandburg did not see Chicago until he was eighteen. As a boy, though, he had delivered and read Chicago newspapers, and the midwestern metropolis fascinated and lured him. When his father secured a railroad pass for his son, who was then taking one dead-end job after another, Sandburg finally got a taste of the big city. He wrote about that first visit in *Always the Young Strangers*. Sandburg's Socialist friend John Sjodin, who had lived in Chicago, told him how to live cheaply in the city by the big lake. And live cheaply he did. In his three days there, he spent twenty-five cents a night for a room in a flophouse, five cents for breakfast, and ten cents each for lunch and dinner. He went to a variety show two nights, but mostly he walked and observed city life: "I . . . never got tired of the roar of the streets, the trolley cars, the teamsters, the drays, buggies, surries, and phaetons, the delivery wagons high with boxes, the brewery wagons piled with barrels. . . ." On his last day in Chicago, he went into a saloon for the free lunch there, paid his five cents for a beer, and while he was "feeding his face" he was approached by a prostitute, who asked him, "Looking fer a good time?" After an exchange of words, Sandburg finally told her, "You're up the wrong alley, sister. I ain't got but two nickels and they wouldn't do you any good." He saw Chicago for one dollar and fifty cents, and much of what he saw would later be reflected time after time in his poetry about the Windy City.

In 1912 Sandburg moved to Chicago and grew to know intimately the places he described in *Chicago Poems*. He worked as a newspaper reporter, haunting Chicago's streets, cafés, and saloons and venturing into the world of prostitutes, working men and women, bums, and radicals. His memorable poem "Chicago" grew out of his overview of the city and its citizens. As his knowledge of "his" Chicago deepened, he wrote such poems as "The Windy City" and "The People, Yes," No. 81, which, though never as widely read as "Chicago," reflect Sandburg's special insights and deserve careful reading. The first section in this anthology brings together his best known and less well known poems about Chicago.

Early in his Chicago days Sandburg had become aware of the Imagists. He admired Emily Dickinson's poetry; he corresponded with Ezra Pound (then touting the Imagist movement); and he befriended and carried on an extended correspondence with Amy Lowell, one of the most prominent of the Imagists. Sandburg was never a member of that coterie, but he did write poems using Imagist techniques as defined by Harriet Monroe, the editor of *Poetry* magazine: the elimination of "every unnecessary word, every unstructural ornament" and the use of concrete images. His best known of these poems, "Fog," was what he called a "free-going, independent American Hoku" [haiku].

Sandburg, with his strong social conscience, at times turned from "pure" images, in poems such as "Fog," to those with a realistic social context. In "Painted Fishes," for example, the beautiful green fishes on a red-lacquered tray, with the paint wearing away from their fins, are placed in a saloon setting. No stranger to saloons, Sandburg creates a beautiful picture out of the sawdust-floored, raucous world of bars.

With Ezra Pound, Amy Lowell, and other Imagists, Sandburg shared an interest in Asian poetry and paintings. At Amy Lowell's home in Massachusetts he met the translator Florence Ayscough. Enthusiastic about her Chinese translations, he transformed some of them into free verse. In "These Valleys Seem Old" he combined Imagism and social criticism. When he later wrote Amy Lowell about permission to print these poems, she responded, in September of 1919, that while Ayscough thought the poems were beautiful, she did not find the renderings exact and would therefore not grant permission. The four poems in "These Valleys Seem Old," inexact renditions though they may be, are as beautiful as the scenes on Chinese scroll paintings. Because of Ayscough's objections, however, they remained unpublished until 1993, when they appeared in *Billy Sunday and Other Poems*.

Sandburg published the "pure" image poems during his lifetime, but most of those with a social context were published posthumously. He may have withheld the latter poems because of Amy Lowell's objections to what she considered "propaganda" in his early poetry. Though Sandburg chose not to publish some of these poems, they are fully as strong as the "pure" ones and are certainly worthy of serious study.

POEMS OF PROTEST

This section contains some of Sandburg's strongest poems of protest, many of which were published after his death. The first of these, "Billy Sunday," appeared in an expurgated form in *Chicago Poems* under the title "To a Contemporary Bunkshooter." The original version played a key role in the publication of this first volume of Sandburg's poetry. In January of 1916 Sandburg sent the manuscript of *Chicago Poems* to Alfred Harcourt, then a young editor at Henry Holt. Harcourt was impressed with the poetry and wanted to publish it, but he knew there would be difficulty in getting some of the text approved by senior members of the publishing firm. He wrote Sandburg: "For obvious reasons, we think the poems, the subjects of which are living people referred to by name, should certainly be omitted. Some of the poems are a little too 'raw'." Sandburg wanted all of his poems published, and he made changes to ensure that they were acceptable. The Billy Sunday poem was retitled, the evangelist Sunday was no longer referred to by name, and language thought to be offensive was removed. Sandburg wrote Harcourt, on February 4, 1916, that the revisions should make it acceptable "to all but the most hidebound and creed-drilled religionists." With Sandburg's revisions, it did appear in *Chicago Poems*. Sandburg was portraying a popular religious figure he considered a pious fraud, and it is not surprising that the original "Billy Sunday," included here, is much more powerful and provocative than the expurgated version in *Chicago Poems*.

The second poem, "The *Eastland*," about the sinking of a steam-ship in the Chicago River, was apparently never offered for publication, perhaps because Sandburg realized that in 1915, when it was written, it was too "raw" for any editor to accept. The *Eastland* was loaded with about twenty-five hundred workers and their families who were being "treated" to a company picnic by their employer when it sank, on July 24, 1915, drowning more than eight hundred. Sandburg, in an essay in the September 1915 issue of the *International Socialist Review*, wrote that government officials had been derelict in their duty for allowing "a cranky, unstable ancient hoodoo tub like the *Eastland*" to sail. It was his belief that "grim industrial feudalism stands with dripping and red hands behind the whole *Eastland* affair." In the poem itself, Sandburg shifted his focus to portray sharply the human misery he saw daily in the lives of working people in the industrialized Chicago he knew so well.

Several of the shorter poems in this section which were published in *Chicago Poems*—"Anna Imroth," "Child of the Romans," "'Boes,'" and others—are particularly powerful. Others, such as "Taking on Suds Men Talk," convey equally strong messages of protest, but again, as with "The *Eastland*," Sandburg probably recognized that they would be unacceptable to editors of that time. For whatever reason, most of his protest poetry about the treatment of women and their deplorable lives in the Chicago he knew went unpublished until 1993.

The last poem in this section, "Legal Midnight Hour," though obviously written immediately after the execution of Sacco and Vanzetti in 1927, also remained unpublished until 1993. The two Italian-born anarchists living in Massachusetts were arrested in 1920 and charged with the murder of two men in a payroll holdup. They were tried, convicted, and executed. It was widely believed in the liberal circles in which Sandburg moved that they were convicted because of their anarchistic beliefs, that they were found guilty in a kangaroo court, and that the evidence against them was tainted or faked. The

Chicago *Daily News,* where Sandburg was employed all through the 1920s, devoted thousands of column inches to the celebrated case, which mesmerized people around the world. With his series of question marks at the end of the poem Sandburg indicated that the controversy would not die after their execution, as, indeed, it has not.

LOVE POEMS

During his courtship of Lilian Steichen, sister of the photographer Edward Steichen and the woman he was to marry in June of 1908, Sandburg sent her his poem "Dream Girl":

> You will come one day in a waver of love,
> Tender as dew, impetuous as rain,
> The tan of the sun will be on your skin,
> The purr of the breeze in your murmuring speech,
> You will pose with a hill-flower grace.
>
> You will come, with your slim, expressive arms,
> A poise of the head no sculptor has caught
> And nuances spoken with shoulder and neck,
> Your face in a pass-and-repass of moods
> As many as skies in delicate change
> Of cloud and blue and flimmering sun.
>
> Yet,
> You may not come, O girl of a dream,
> We may but pass as the world goes by
> And take from a look of eyes into eyes,
> A film of hope and a memoried day.

Lilian responded, on February 15, 1908: "Your *Dream Girl . . .* is indeed a dream girl—not of our world to-day but of the Millennial Epoch of Rest. In our Epoch of Struggle girls must be made of sterner stuff." She continued, "So while I have no praise for the *Dream Girl* itself (from the standpoint of democratic art)—yet I have plenty of appreciation for the intelligence that created it—for the powers for good in that intelligence when employed in socialist propaganda!" Lilian Steichen was a brilliant woman and a major influence in improving Sandburg's poetry; indeed, many of the poems in his early volumes owe much of their power to her careful work as his major artistic critic.

After he met Lilian, whom he called Paula, Sandburg's love poetry took on a dramatic intensity. He wrote clearly and lovingly about her and their children, Margaret, Janet, and Helga.

Sandburg wrote other love poems of great passion, poems he did not attempt to publish. Some of these—"In Blue Gown and In Black Satin Gown," "She Held Herself a Deep Pool for Him," "An Interwoven Man and Woman Talked," "Troth Tryst," and "Hellcat"— remained unpublished until 1993. Just why Sandburg chose not to publish them in his lifetime is unknown. Perhaps he thought them too passionate, exposing an inner self he wished to keep hidden.

"Bilbea," the final love poem here, is in a class all to itself. As Sandburg explained in *The World of Carl Sandburg:* "In some old *National Geographic Magazine* there was an interpretation of Babylonian hieroglyphics of this vintage, by a responsible interpreter, and it said practically the idea expressed in this poem." Again, we do not know what drew Sandburg to this love poem from a Babylonian tablet, but we may speculate that it was its theme, the universality of love.

LINCOLN

By the early 1920s Sandburg was thinking of writing a biography of Lincoln. He wanted to break down all the sentimentalizing about the man he had long admired. Even before he began the biography he wrote a number of poems about Lincoln, and he continued to do so throughout his career. The first part of this section contains those Lincoln poems that Sandburg chose to publish during his lifetime. At the time of his death he had other Lincoln poems in his files, and five of them, arranged together, conclude this section. Three of these have never before appeared in print.

In "Fire-Logs," published in 1918, Sandburg wrote imaginatively about Lincoln's mother, who was thought to have been illegitimate. He presents her as a dreamer, just as her famous son was known to be. In the 1916 poem "In a Back Alley" Lincoln appears as the face on the penny, the lowest denomination of coins, the common currency of the people, which newsboys are carelessly pitching for idle amusement. "Knucks," published in 1918, is a startling image of contrast between the businessman in Lincoln's home town who sells iron knuckles for fighting and Lincoln, whose message is "malice to none."

By the time The People, Yes was published in 1936, Sandburg was a mature biographer and was well on the way toward completing his life of Lincoln. He had spent years researching, thinking, and writing about the Great Emancipator. The long Lincoln poem here, No. 57 of The People, Yes, is an overview of the president and is studded with his quotes. It shows him as a humorist, democrat, philosopher, historian, poet, man of the common man, leader of the people.

"The Long Shadow of Lincoln: A Litany" was written during the dark days of World War II. Sandburg for many years had been conscious of Lincoln's "long shadow," which compelled him to draw parallels between Lincoln and Roosevelt. He wrote President Roosevelt, on March 29, 1935, that he was starting the final volume of the Lincoln biography and that his eyes and ears were in two eras: "You are the best light of democracy that has occupied the White House since Lincoln. You have set in motion trends that to many are banners of dawn." Sandburg also saw the long shadow of Lincoln cast over Roosevelt's leadership in World War II, from 1941 to 1945.

The earliest of the five poems about Lincoln that Sandburg did not publish is dated 1914 and titled "Abraham Lincoln's Father and Mother." It shows Sandburg's early thinking as a biographer. He knew that questions had been raised about the legitimacy of Lincoln's mother, Nancy Hanks. William Herndon, Lincoln's law partner, said Lincoln had told him that Nancy Hanks was illegitimate, the daughter of "a well-bred Virginia farmer or planter." According to Herndon, Lincoln believed that "his power of analysis, his logic, his mental activity, his ambition" came from his unknown grandfather. That Lincoln's mother was illegitimate is now widely accepted by scholars.

Sandburg also knew from his reading that doubt had been cast on Lincoln's own legitimacy. Herndon thought that the questions about Lincoln's paternity "were an outgrowth of the campaign of 1860." However accurate that speculation might be, over the years at least seven men were alleged to have been the father of Abraham Lincoln. Six years after Sandburg wrote "Abraham Lincoln's Father and Mother," William E. Barton demolished all such rumors and allegations in *The Paternity of Abraham Lincoln*. It is now accepted as fact that Thomas Lincoln was the father of Abraham.

While Sandburg was aware of the rumors about Thomas and Nancy Hanks Lincoln, his writings about them were intended to be poetic, not factual. Later, as a biographer, he would insist on more substantial facts, though even in the biography his presentation of Lincoln, his family, and his times would remain poetic.

Two of the poems—"Lincoln" and "Mr. Lincoln and His Gloves"—appear to have a common source. In 1861, on his way to Washington for his inauguration, Lincoln appeared in New York at the Verdi opera *A Masked Ball* wearing black gloves instead of the more fashionable white ones. Because of the black gloves, Lincoln's large hands, and his shambling gait, a hostile press immediately dubbed him a "gorilla" and a "baboon."

"Lincoln," written in 1915, after the beginning of World War I, was in an envelope of poems Sandburg labeled "to be published after my death." In this poem Sandburg uses the baboon imagery in a fantastic vein, picking up wild jungle scenes, with Lincoln's hands as a constant, and transforming all into the horror of war. In the jungle, where hyenas "rip the guts of babies," he re-creates a place of savagery similar to the battlegrounds in the United States during the Civil War and even more similar to those of the European war being waged at that time. Lincoln, now with a baboon face, sings a song to himself, a song the rest of us cannot understand, praying for a gateway, a return to civilized behavior. Like Lincoln with his large hands, the baboon sits with "hands the same as always."

"Mr. Lincoln and His Gloves" was written for dramatic reading by the French refugee Marianne Lorraine, and she performed it widely in the United States, but the poem did not appear in print until Margaret Sandburg published it in *Breathing Tokens* in 1978. The poem begins with the incident in February of 1861 when New York socialites laughed at Lincoln with his black gloves at the opera. Sandburg chronicles Lincoln's travails with gloves, sometimes joking about them, just as Lincoln did.

In 1915 Sandburg wrote "Journey and Oath," a poem that begins dramatically with an account of Lincoln's death and the journey of his body back to Illinois. Unfortunately, the remainder of the poem does not live up to the promise of the first lines. In trying to present poetically the reaction of "this man and that" to Lincoln's murder, Sandburg resorts to bombast, and the forced oath is unconvincing. He did not publish the poem, but Margaret Sandburg included it in *Breathing Tokens*.

The final poem in this section was also in the envelope Sandburg labeled "to be published after my death." It is untitled, but its content suggests that it was written at the same time as "Lincoln." The jungle and the gorilla imagery are there, though this time they are woven into the "mystery" of evolution. Sandburg is facing a question any biographer and reader of Lincoln must raise: How did Lincoln become Lincoln? How did this giant of history evolve "out of the slime of the sea," out of the jungle? Sandburg invites the reader to see a "mystery without end."

Just why did Sandburg leave these poems unpublished? There are no easy answers. With "Abraham Lincoln's Father and Mother," he may have felt uneasy about reprinting rumors and speculations on illegitimacy. Or he may have thought the poem needed explanatory footnotes to be fully understood, and as a poet who spoke directly to his readers, Sandburg objected to such academic paraphernalia. The latter explanation may also be applied to "Lincoln" and to the untitled poem, both of which were intended to be published only after Sandburg's death. When he was under the sod, others would or could provide the glosses to his poems. As for "Journey and Oath," he may have realized that the poem needed revision, put it aside for later work, and never returned to it. And it is entirely possible that Sandburg may have lost or forgotten "Mr. Lincoln and His Gloves." But these are only speculations. There are no clues among Sandburg's voluminous papers to help explain why these five poems did not appear in print in his lifetime.

ANTI-WAR AND WAR POEMS

From the time he was a boy, Carl Sandburg was aware of anti-war sentiments. His father's cousin had left Sweden to avoid military service and also refused to serve in the Union Army, for he "couldn't take a hand in killing men." Sandburg in his youth did not share this view; he was fascinated by the Civil War and its generals. When the Spanish-American War began, in 1898, he was working as an apprentice to a painter. Lured by the war propaganda, he joined

Company C, Sixth Infantry Regiment of the Illinois Volunteers. He was, of course, also looking for travel and adventure. Instead, he found considerable misery.

During his college years Sandburg was introduced to Socialist ideas, and his radical views developed before the beginning of World War I. He had served as a Socialist organizer, and both he and his wife, Lilian, saw war as a folly promulgated by capitalists and national rulers. The earliest poems in this section, including "Buttons" and "Murmurings in a Field Hospital," show Sandburg's strong anti-war bias in the beginning years of the war. He was probably unable to publish some of his anti-war poems, such as "Planked Whitefish," because of their brutal imagery and language.

When the United States entered the war in 1917, however, Sandburg and his wife broke with the anti-war Socialists. Sandburg later served as a war correspondent in Sweden, and he propagandized for the war in such poems as "The Four Brothers." This poem, though immensely popular at the time, lacks the strong passion of his earlier anti-war poems.

With the rise of Fascism and Nazism during the 1930s, Sandburg's sympathies were with the Loyalists in the Spanish Civil War. His "Nearer Than Any Mother's Heart Wishes," written during this period, reflects his deep concern for the human tragedies of war, although it was not published in his lifetime.

During World War II Sandburg propagandized for the Allies in such poems as "Open Letter to the Poet Archibad MacLeish Who Has Forsaken His Massachusetts Farm to Make Propaganda for Freedom" and "The Man with the Broken Fingers." Though still opposed to war, with its senseless and deadly violence, Sandburg felt he had no choice but to support the Allied effort against what he saw as the greater evil of the Nazis and Fascists.

In the final poem in this section, "Grass," a work often anthologized, Sandburg, writing of the grass covering the graves of soldiers used as "cannon fodder," shows his sympathy for those who fought and were killed as well as his knowledge of Nature's relentlessness.

PORTRAITS

An acute observer of people around him and an avid student of history, Sandburg read Browning's masterful poetic portraits when he was a student at Lombard College and was also influenced by Edgar Lee Masters's word portraits in *Spoon River Anthology*. Moreover, Sandburg was a journalist interested in writing about people, and the poems in this section show his deftness at characterization.

These poetic portraits range from pieces on Philip Green Wright, a professor at Lombard College who was one of the major early influences on Sandburg's life and art, to Napoleon, Eugene Debs, Amy Lowell, Nathaniel Hawthorne, John Milton, Ezra Pound, Charlie Chaplin, and the Sandburg dog Dan. These vivid character studies, written in simple language, attempt to get to the essence of the person (or dog) being written about.

AFRICAN-AMERICANS

In his constant concern about the poor and disinherited in American society, Sandburg often wrote about African-Americans. This section contains a selection of these poems, several of which are dramatic portraits. They are wide-ranging in content, from "Jazz Fantasia," reflecting the poet's interest in music; to the fiery words of the ex-slave Sojourner Truth; to a folk prayer from Lang Syne Plantation in South Carolina; to a short poem about a simple woman called Cleo with her poetical evocation of angels; to the prophetess standing on Chicago street corners warning of destruction; to the much-abused Elizabeth Umpstead; and, finally, to the pro-union man Henry Stephens. In this series of portraits of African-Americans, common folk living in both country and urban settings, Sandburg shows some of them content with their lives and others defiant. Together, these poems offer stunning and diverse images of African-Americans.

In his pamphlet on the 1919 Chicago race riots and in the poem "Hoodlums" (included in the Poems of Protest section), Sandburg wrote about this terrible episode in Chicago history, in which thirty-eight people died, fifteen whites and twenty-three blacks. He understood the part that poverty played in white hatred and fear of African-Americans, and he knew that government did not protect its citizens of color. He wrote, "On the one hand we have blind lawless government failing to function through policemen ignorant of Lincoln, the Civil War, the Emancipation Proclamation, and a theory sanctioned and baptized in a storm of red blood. . . . And on the other hand we have a gaunt involuntary poverty from which issues the hoodlum."

Sandburg denounced white hoodlums in "Man, the Man-Hunter." This unexpurgated poem about a lynching was sent to Louis Untermeyer in 1920 for inclusion in his anthology *An American Miscellany*. Afraid that the language in the poem would offend both church groups and the Society for the Suppression of Vice, Untermeyer asked Sandburg to make revisions. Sandburg agreed to remove the offending language, but he wrote Untermeyer in March 1920:

> . . . it's come over me clear the last two or three years that in a group killing of a man, in a mobbing, the event reaches a point where all rationale is gone; such a term as "anarchist" and "traitor" or "Boche" or "Englander Schwein" disappears and they babble hysterically only one or two epithets, in our language usually a tenor of "Son of a Bitch" with a bass of "Cocksucker." Since some of the finest blood of the human family goes this way poets and painters have a right to try to employ it or at least not kid themselves about what actually

happened at Golgotha. Since I've talked with men who were in the trenches and since I've seen race riots I am suspicious that the sponge of vinegar on the spear is a faked legend and what probably happened, if the historicity of Jesus is ever established, is that they cut off his genital organ and stuck it in his mouth. . . .

These poems show in vivid detail a Sandburg far ahead of his time in his passionate concern for the plight of individual African-Americans and for race relations overall throughout the United States.

POET OF THE PEOPLE

In her biography of Sandburg, Penelope Niven wrote that with the publication of *Chicago Poems* a "wide audience was beginning to listen" to Sandburg. "He offended many," she noted, "but the poems spoke in new ways to readers who still equated rhyme and romanticism with poetry." Sandburg used free verse and wrote realistically about the world he saw, but in the years following *Chicago Poems* he offended fewer and fewer people. His radicalism was less pronounced, and he identified more and more with the people, the mob. Over decades, he took his poetry and his music directly to the people through countless appearances across the country. In the minds of most Americans, he was finally seen as a character and an entertainer—certainly not as a dangerous radical.

The poems in this section are diverse in form, content, and length, but throughout there is a spirit of "the people, yes," a phrase Sandburg eventually used as the title of one of his most characteristic volumes of poetry. In his resounding "Yes" he showed his deep indebtedness to Whitman, whose "Song of Myself" begins:

I celebrate myself, and sing myself,
And what I assume you shall assume,
For every atom belonging to me as good belongs to you.

Sandburg was no less egotistical than Whitman: he believed that the people would assume what he assumed. Like Whitman, he sang himself and the people, and in his best poems they became one. "I am the people, the mob," he would chant, and he would join the mob in the cities and in the country, in their happiness, sadness, and tragedies. His concern eventually was for the family of man, and he became in "Timesweep" a part of everything that had ever existed:

> There is only one Maker in the world
> and His children cover the earth
> and they are named All God's Children.

MUSINGS

Sandburg the dreamer often wrote down his poetic musings; some of the most interesting and provocative of these are presented here. While Sandburg was at times gregarious, he was also introspective, given to dreams and speculations. Imagine the poet sitting by his window at the newspaper office or in his study at home, lost in thought, musing about himself, his world, about poetry and art, about the human condition. The poems that spring from these quiet moments are sometimes comic, sometimes sardonic, sometimes serious. In "Chicago Poet" he looked in the mirror and "saluted a nobody." In "Wilderness" he was animalistic and also a singer of songs. In "I Should Like to Be Hanged on a Summer Afternoon" he imagined his own death. He gave academic critics (most of whom scorned him) their due in "The Abracadabra Boys." As always, Sandburg wanted his musings, even the personal ones, to be understood by his readers, who he assumed had dreams and musings that were similar to his own.

POETRY DEFINITIONS

In his famous definition of Metaphysical poetry Dr. Samuel Johnson spoke of "heterogeneous ideas" being "yoked by violence together."

Sandburg was not, of course, a Metaphysical poet, but in the thirty-eight definitions of poetry found in this section he does yoke disparate ideas together, sometimes violently, in order to suggest some of the mystery of poetry.

Writing about these "Tentative (First Model) Definitions of Poetry" in his critical study *Carl Sandburg*, Richard Crowder says that Sandburg "used imagery of all sorts to explain this paradoxical entwining of available material and the ultimately inexpressible. The best known of these thrusts into the dark called poetry is a combination of 'hyacinths and biscuits,' dreams and flowers, yes, but practicalities and words, too. Language is frightening and awesome in its flexibility, connotations, and emotional impact, but it is the material substance ('biscuits') which a poet must use to try to communicate the ineffable ('hyacinths')."

Sandburg would undoubtedly have rejected Crowder's analysis—and, indeed, would probably have rejected all formal analyses of his poetry—preferring instead the informal interpretations of individual readers. He wanted his definitions to reflect the mystery of poetry. Sandburg believed "what can be explained is not poetry."

"All my life," Sandburg wrote in the last paragraph of his "Notes for a Preface" to his *Complete Poems*, "I have been trying to learn to read, to see and hear, and to write." He says he had over many decades "written by different methods and in a wide miscellany of moods" and still he favored "simple poems . . . which continue to have an appeal for simple people."

A Note on the Text

The texts of the poems are as published in *The Complete Poems of Carl Sandburg, Breathing Tokens, Billy Sunday and Other Poems*, and *The World of Carl Sandburg*. Except in one case, all the ellipses are Sandburg's; this exception has been noted by the use of square brackets.

The previously unpublished poems about Lincoln were transcribed from manuscripts in the Sandburg Collection in the Library of the University of Illinois at Urbana-Champaign.

Selected Poems

CHICAGO

Here is the difference between Dante, Milton and me. They wrote about hell and never saw the place. I wrote about Chicago after looking the town over for years and years.

— CARL SANDBURG, from *Carl Sandburg:
A Pictorial Biography*

I admit there is some animus of violence in Chicago Poems but the aim was rather the presentation of motives and character than the furtherance of I.W.W. theories. Of course, I honestly prefer the theories of the I.W.W. to those of its opponents and some of my honest preferences may have crept into the book, as you suggest, but the aim was to sing, blab, chortle, yodel, like people, and people in the sense of human beings subtracted from formal doctrines.

— CARL SANDBURG, from a letter to Amy Lowell,
circa June 1917

❧ *Chicago*

Hog Butcher for the World,
Tool Maker, Stacker of Wheat,
Player with Railroads and the Nation's Freight Handler;
Stormy, husky, brawling,
City of the Big Shoulders:

They tell me you are wicked and I believe them, for I have seen
    your painted women under the gas lamps luring the farm boys.
And they tell me you are crooked and I answer: Yes, it is true I have
    seen the gunman kill and go free to kill again.
And they tell me you are brutal and my reply is: On the faces of
    women and children I have seen the marks of wanton hunger.
And having answered so I turn once more to those who sneer at this
    my city, and I give them back the sneer and say to them:
Come and show me another city with lifted head singing so proud
    to be alive and coarse and strong and cunning.
Flinging magnetic curses amid the toil of piling job on job, here is a
    tall bold slugger set vivid against the little soft cities;
Fierce as a dog with tongue lapping for action, cunning as a savage
    pitted against the wilderness,
    Bareheaded,
    Shoveling,
    Wrecking,
    Planning,
    Building, breaking, rebuilding,
Under the smoke, dust all over his mouth, laughing with white teeth,
Under the terrible burden of destiny laughing as a young man laughs,

Laughing even as an ignorant fighter laughs who has never lost a
  battle,
Bragging and laughing that under his wrist is the pulse, and under
  his ribs the heart of the people,
  Laughing!
Laughing the stormy, husky, brawling laughter of Youth, half-
  naked, sweating, proud to be Hog Butcher, Tool Maker, Stacker
  of Wheat, Player with Railroads and Freight Handler to the
  Nation.

Halsted Street Car

Come you, cartoonists,
Hang on a strap with me here
At seven o'clock in the morning
On a Halsted street car.

  Take your pencils
  And draw these faces.

Try with your pencils for these crooked faces,
That pig-sticker in one corner—his mouth—
That overall factory girl—her loose cheeks.

  Find for your pencils
  A way to mark your memory
  Of tired empty faces.

  After their night's sleep,
  In the moist dawn

And cool daybreak,
    Faces
Tired of wishes,
Empty of dreams.

❧ *The Workingmen*

In the dusk of the dawn they go
A hundred thousand feet sluffing the sidewalks
Setting a dull-rumbling hum up the streets of the city.

❧ *Fish Crier*

I know a Jew fish crier down on Maxwell Street with a voice like a
    north wind blowing over corn stubble in January.
He dangles herring before prospective customers evincing a joy
    identical with that of Pavlowa dancing.
His face is that of a man terribly glad to be selling fish, terribly glad
    that God made fish, and customers to whom he may call his
    wares from a pushcart.

❧ *Muckers*

Twenty men stand watching the muckers.
    Stabbing the sides of the ditch
    Where clay gleams yellow,
    Driving the blades of their shovels

Deeper and deeper for the new gas mains,
  Wiping sweat off their faces
    With red bandanas.

The muckers work on . . . pausing . . . to pull
Their boots out of suckholes where they slosh.

  Of the twenty looking on
Ten murmur, "O, it's a hell of a job,"
Ten others, "Jesus, I wish I had the job."

❧ Mill-Doors

  You never come back.
I say good-by when I see you going in the doors,
The hopeless open doors that call and wait
And take you then for—how many cents a day?
How many cents for the sleepy eyes and fingers?

I say good-by because I know they tap your wrists,
In the dark, in the silence, day by day,
And all the blood of you drop by drop,
And you are old before you are young.
  You never come back.

❧ Mag

I wish to God I never saw you, Mag.
I wish you never quit your job and came along with me.
I wish we never bought a license and a white dress

For you to get married in the day we ran off to a minister
And told him we would love each other and take care of each other
Always and always long as the sun and the rain lasts anywhere.
Yes, I'm wishing now you lived somewhere away from here
And I was a bum on the bumpers a thousand miles away dead
    broke.
        I wish the kids had never come
        And rent and coal and clothes to pay for
        And a grocery man calling for cash,
        Every day cash for beans and prunes.
        I wish to God I never saw you, Mag.
        I wish to God the kids had never come.

❧ Onion Days

Mrs. Gabrielle Giovannitti comes along Peoria Street every morning
    at nine o'clock
With kindling wood piled on top of her head, her eyes looking
    straight ahead to find the way for her old feet.
Her daughter-in-law, Mrs. Pietro Giovannitti, whose husband was
    killed in a tunnel explosion through the negligence of a fellow-
    servant,
Works ten hours a day, sometimes twelve, picking onions for Jasper
    on the Bowmanville road.
She takes a street car at half-past five in the morning, Mrs. Pietro
    Giovannitti does,
And gets back from Jasper's with cash for her day's work, between
    nine and ten o'clock at night.
Last week she got eight cents a box, Mrs. Pietro Giovannitti, picking
    onions for Jasper,

But this week Jasper dropped the pay to six cents a box because so many women and girls were answering the ads in the *Daily News.*

Jasper belongs to an Episcopal church in Ravenswood and on certain Sundays

He enjoys chanting the Nicene creed with his daughters on each side of him joining their voices with his.

If the preacher repeats old sermons of a Sunday, Jasper's mind wanders to his 700-acre farm and how he can make it produce more efficiently

And sometimes he speculates on whether he could word an ad in the *Daily News* so it would bring more women and girls out to his farm and reduce operating costs.

Mrs. Pietro Giovannitti is far from desperate about life; her joy is in a child she knows will arrive to her in three months.

And now while these are the pictures for today there are other pictures of the Giovannitti people I could give you for tomorrow,

And how some of them go to the county agent on winter mornings with their baskets for beans and cornmeal and molasses.

I listen to fellows saying here's good stuff for a novel or it might be worked up into a good play.

I say there's no dramatist living can put old Mrs. Gabrielle Giovannitti into a play with that kindling wood piled on top of her head coming along Peoria Street nine o'clock in the morning.

Dynamiter

I sat with a dynamiter at supper in a German saloon eating steak and onions.

And he laughed and told stories of his wife and children and the cause of labor and the working class.

It was laughter of an unshakable man knowing life to be a rich and red-blooded thing.

Yes, his laugh rang like the call of gray birds filled with a glory of joy ramming their winged flight through a rain storm.

His name was in many newspapers as an enemy of the nation and few keepers of churches or schools would open their doors to him.

Over the steak and onions not a word was said of his deep days and nights as a dynamiter.

Only I always remember him as a lover of life, a lover of children, a lover of all free, reckless laughter everywhere—lover of red hearts and red blood the world over.

❧ *Mamie*

Mamie beat her head against the bars of a little Indiana town and dreamed of romance and big things off somewhere the way the railroad trains all ran.

She could see the smoke of the engines get lost down where the streaks of steel flashed in the sun and when the newspapers came in on the morning mail she knew there was a big Chicago far off, where all the trains ran.

She got tired of the barber shop boys and the post office chatter and the church gossip and the old pieces the band played on the Fourth of July and Decoration Day

And sobbed at her fate and beat her head against the bars and was going to kill herself

When the thought came to her that if she was going to die she might as well die struggling for a clutch of romance among the streets of Chicago.

She has a job now at six dollars a week in the basement of the Boston Store

And even now she beats her head against the bars in the same old
   way and wonders of there is a bigger place the railroads run to
   from Chicago where maybe there is

> romance
> and big things
> and real dreams
> that never go smash.

 *Working Girls*

The working girls in the morning are going to work—long lines of
   them afoot amid the downtown stores and factories, thousands
   with little brick-shaped lunches wrapped in newspapers under
   their arms.
Each morning as I move through this river of young-woman life I
   feel a wonder about where it is all going, so many with a peach
   bloom of young years on them and laughter of red lips and
   memories in their eyes of dances the night before and plays and
   walks.
Green and gray streams run side by side in a river and so here are
   always the others, those who have been over the way, the women
   who know each one the end of life's gamble for her, the meaning
   and the clue, the how and the why of the dances and the arms
   that passed around their waists and the fingers that played in their
   hair.
Faces go by written over: "I know it all, I know where the bloom
   and the laughter go and I have memories," and the feet of these
   move slower and they have wisdom where the others have
   beauty.
So the green and the gray move in the early morning on the down-
   town streets.

✤ Trafficker

Among the shadows where two streets cross,
A woman lurks in the dark and waits
To move on when a policeman heaves in view.
Smiling a broken smile from a face
Painted over haggard bones and desperate eyes,
All night she offers passers-by what they will
Of her beauty wasted, body faded, claims gone,
And no takers.

✤ Harrison Street Court

I heard a woman's lips
Speaking to a companion
Say these words:

"A woman what hustles
Never keeps nothin'
For all her hustlin'.
Somebody always gets
What she goes on the street for.
If it ain't a pimp
It's a bull what gets it.
I been hustlin' now
Till I ain't much good any more.
I got nothin' to show for it.

Some man got it all,
Every night's hustlin' I ever did."

🌺 *Gone*

Everybody loved Chick Lorimer in our town.
        Far off
        Everybody loved her.
So we all love a wild girl keeping a hold
        On a dream she wants.
Nobody knows now where Chick Lorimer went.
Nobody knows why she packed her trunk . . . a few old things
And is gone,
        Gone with her little chin
        Thrust ahead of her
        And her soft hair blowing careless
        From under a wide hat,
Dancer, singer, a laughing passionate lover.

Were there ten men or a hundred hunting Chick?
Were there five men or fifty with aching hearts?
        Everybody loved Chick Lorimer.
        Nobody knows where she's gone.

🌿 Soiled Dove

Let us be honest; the lady was not a harlot until she married a corporation lawyer who picked her from a Ziegfeld chorus.

Before then she never took anybody's money and paid for her silk stockings out of what she earned singing and dancing.

She loved one man and he loved six women and the game was changing her looks, calling for more and more massage money and high coin for the beauty doctors.

Now she drives a long, underslung motor car all by herself, reads in the day's papers what her husband is doing to the inter-state commerce commission, requires a larger corsage from year to year, and wonders sometimes how one man is coming along with six women.

🌿 Old Woman

The owl-car clatters along, dogged by the echo
From building and battered paving-stone;
The headlight scoffs at the mist
And fixes its yellow rays in the cold slow rain;
Against a pane I press my forehead
And drowsily look on the walls and sidewalks.

The headlight finds the way
And life is gone from the wet and the welter—
Only an old woman, bloated, disheveled and bleared

Far-wandered waif of other days,
Huddles for sleep in a doorway,
Homeless.

❧ *Washerwoman*

The washerwoman is a member of the Salvation Army.
And over the tub of suds rubbing underwear clean
She sings that Jesus will wash her sins away
And the red wrongs she has done God and man
Shall be white as driven snow.
Rubbing underwear she sings of the Last Great Washday.

❧ *Gypsy Mother*

In a hole-in-a-wall on Halsted Street sits a gypsy woman,
In a garish gas-lit rendezvous, in a humpback higgling hole-in-a-wall.

The left hand is a tattler; stars and oaths and alphabets
Commit themselves and tell happenings gone, happenings to come,
    pathways of honest people, hypocrites.

"Long pointed fingers mean imagination; a star on the third finger
    says a black shadow walks near."
Cross the gypsy's hand with fifty cents and she takes your left hand
    and reads how you shall be happy in love, or not, and whether
    you die rich, or not.
Signs outside the hole-in-a-wall say so, misspell the promises, scrawl
    the superior gypsy mysteries.

A red shawl on her shoulders falls with a fringe hem to a green skirt;
Chains of yellow beads sweep from her neck to her tawny hands.
Fifty springtimes must have kissed her mouth holding a calabash
　　pipe.
She pulls slow contemplative puffs of smoke; she is a shape for
　　ghosts of contemplation to sit around and ask why something
　　cheap as happiness is here and more besides, chapped lips, rough
　　eyes, red shawl.
She is thinking about somebody and something the same as Whis-
　　tler's mother sat and thought about somebody and something.

In a hole-in-a-wall on Halsted Street are stars, oaths, alphabets.

🐝 *Implications*

When the charge of election bribery was brought against an Illinois
senator, he replied, "I read the Bible and believe it from cover to
cover."

When his accusers specified five hundred dollars of corruption
money was paid in a St. Louis hotel bathroom, his friends answered,
"He is faithful to his wife and always kind to his children."

When he was ousted from the national senate and the doors of his
bank were closed by government receivers and a grand jury indicted
him, he took the vows of an old established church.

When a jury acquitted him of guilt as a bank wrecker, following the
testimony of prominent citizens that he was an honest man, he issued
a statement to the public for the newspapers, proclaiming he knew
beforehand no jury would darken the future of an honest man with
an unjust verdict.

Graceland

Tomb of a millionaire,
A multi-millionaire, ladies and gentlemen,
Place of the dead where they spend every year
The usury of twenty-five thousand dollars
    For upkeep and flowers
To keep fresh the memory of the dead.
The merchant prince gone to dust
Commanded in his written will
Over the signed name of his last testament
Twenty-five thousand dollars be set aside
For roses, lilacs, hydrangeas, tulips,
For perfume and color, sweetness of remembrance
Around his last long home.

(A hundred cash girls want nickels to go to the movies tonight.
In the back stalls of a hundred saloons, women are at tables
Drinking with men or waiting for men jingling loose silver dollars
    in their pockets.
In a hundred furnished rooms is a girl who sells silk or dress goods
    or leather stuff for six dollars a week wages
And when she pulls on her stockings in the morning she is reckless
    about God and the newspapers and the police, the talk of her
    home town or the name people call her.)

❧ *Skyscraper*

By day the skyscraper looms in the smoke and sun and has a soul.

Prairie and valley, streets of the city, pour people into it and they mingle among its twenty floors and are poured out again back to the streets, prairies and valleys.

It is the men and women, boys and girls so poured in and out all day that give the building a soul of dreams and thoughts and memories.

(Dumped in the sea or fixed in a desert, who would care for the building or speak its name or ask a policeman the way to it?)

Elevators slide on their cables and tubes catch letters and parcels and iron pipes carry gas and water in and sewage out.

Wires climb with secrets, carry light and carry words, and tell terrors and profits and loves—curses of men grappling plans of business and questions of women in plots of love.

Hour by hour the caissons reach down to the rock of the earth and hold the building to a turning planet.

Hour by hour the girders play as ribs and reach out and hold together the stone walls and floors.

Hour by hour the hand of the mason and the stuff of the mortar clinch the pieces and parts to the shape an architect voted.

Hour by hour the sun and the rain, the air and the rust, and the press of time running into centuries, play on the building inside and out and use it.

Men who sunk the pilings and mixed the mortar are laid in graves where the wind whistles a wild song without words

And so are men who strung the wires and fixed the pipes and tubes
and those who saw it rise floor by floor.
Souls of them all are here, even the hod carrier begging at back
doors hundreds of miles away and the bricklayer who went to
state's prison for shooting another man while drunk.
(One man fell from a girder and broke his neck at the end of a
straight plunge—he is here—his soul has gone into the stones
of the building.)

On the office doors from tier to tier—hundreds of names and each
name standing for a face written across with a dead child, a pas-
sionate lover, a driving ambition for a million dollar business or
a lobster's ease of life.

Behind the signs on the doors they work and the walls tell nothing
from room to room.
Ten-dollar-a-week stenographers take letters from corporation offi-
cers, lawyers, efficiency engineers, and tons of letters go bundled
from the building to all ends of the earth.
Smiles and tears of each office girl go into the soul of the building
just the same as the master-men who rule the building.

Hands of clocks turn to noon hours and each floor empties its men
and women who go away and eat and come back to work.
Toward the end of the afternoon all work slackens and all jobs go
slower as the people feel day closing on them.
One by one the floors are emptied. . . . The uniformed elevator men
are gone. Pails clang. . . . Scrubbers work, talking in foreign
tongues. Broom and water and mop clean from the floors human
dust and spit, and machine grime of the day.
Spelled in electric fire on the roof are words telling miles of houses
and people where to buy a thing for money. The sign speaks till
midnight.

Darkness on the hallways. Voices echo. Silence holds. . . . Watchmen
walk slow from floor to floor and try the doors. Revolvers bulge
from their hip pockets. . . . Steel safes stand in corners. Money is
stacked in them.
A young watchman leans at a window and sees the lights of barges
butting their way across a harbor, nets of red and white lanterns
in a railroad yard, and a span of glooms splashed with lines of
white and blurs of crosses and clusters over the sleeping city.
By night the skyscraper looms in the smoke and the stars and has a
soul.

🌺 *The People, Yes*

81

Chicago seems all fox and swine,
Dreams interfused with smut, dung, hunger.
Yet Chicago is not all belly and mouth and
    overwrought sex and lies and greed
    and snobs.
Chicago has something over and beyond.
Sometime the seeds and cross-fertilizations
    now moving in Chicago may inaugurate
    a crossroads of great gladness.
The same goes for Omaha and points west,
    for Buffalo and points east.

Out of the shopping crowds at State and Madison, hot with bundles
and bargains,
A humpty-dumpty runt of a man dived at high noon into a forest of
rubbernecks craning at a skywriting plane telling you what ciga-
rette to smoke next, what cigarette to buy,

And he came up to say there was too much quick thinking and he
would offer a little slow thinking:

"From the museum mummies I came to these ghosts swirling around
State and Madison, Forty-second and Fifth Avenue, and about all
I learned was this, you can write it on a thumbnail:

"There is a dead past and a blank future and the same humanity is
in each and it's all ham and eggs, dog eat dog, the toughest guts
have their way, and they kill and kill to see who'll get the most
marbles, the most cocoanuts, the most little embossed pieces of
paper."

And then he went on, wiping his chin with four fingers and a thumb,
screwing his eyes to a thin slit, and correcting himself:

"I take that back. Write it off as a loss. If the big arch of the sky
were paper and the violet depths of the sea were ink, I could
never live long enough to write the dreams of man and the
dynamic drive of those dreams.

"Who and what is man? He is Atlas and Thor and Yankee Doodle,
an eagle, a lion, a rooster, a bear that walks like a man, an ele-
phant, a moon-face, David and Goliath, Paul Bunyan and the
Flying Dutchman, Shakespeare, Lincoln and Christ, the Equator
and the Arctic Poles, holding in one hand the Bank of England
and the Roman Catholic Church, in the other the Red Army and
the Standard Oil Company, holding in easy reach the dogs of war
and the doves of peace, the tigers of wrath and the horses of
instruction.

"Let me sell you my dreams. Take these dreams for whatever you
want to pay me. You shall never be tired till the sea is tired. You
shall never go weary till the land and the wind go weary. You
will be hard as nails, soft as blue fog.

"Man is born with rainbows in his heart and you'll never read him
unless you consider rainbows. He is a trouble shooter with big
promises. He trades the Oklahoma roan mustang for a tub in the
sky with wings falling falling in Alaska. Hard as a rock his head

is an egg and ponders ponders. He is a phantasmagoria of crimson dawns and what it takes to build his dreams."

So the finish. He ceased from wiping his chin with four fingers and a thumb, ceased from screwing his eyes to a thin slit, ceased correcting himself.

Then he vanished. In a wreath of blue smoke from a panatella seegar he was gone, a scholar, a clown, and a dreambook seller who had said enough for one day.

Turning a corner he talked to himself about the dust of the knuckles of his great-grandfathers, how they once were hard as nails and could pick a vest-button with a bullet, and how his own little knuckles sometime would shiver into fine dust and how he wanted snowdrifts piled over him and the inscription: HERE NO ONE LIES BURIED.

The Windy City

I

The lean hands of wagon men
put out pointing fingers here,
picked this crossway, put it on a map,
set up their sawbucks, fixed their shotguns,
found a hitching place for the pony express,
made a hitching place for the iron horse,
the one-eyed horse with the fire-spit head,
found a homelike spot and said, "Make a home,"
saw this corner with a mesh of rails, shuttling
    people, shunting cars, shaping the junk of
    the earth to a new city.

The hands of men took hold and tugged
And the breaths of men went into the junk
And the junk stood up into skyscrapers and asked:
Who am I? Am I a city? And if I am what is my name?
And once while the time whistles blew and blew again
The men answered: Long ago we gave you a name,
Long ago we laughed and said: You? Your name is Chicago.

Early the red men gave a name to a river,
    the place of the skunk,
       the river of the wild onion smell,
       Shee-caw-go.

Out of the payday songs of steam shovels,
Out of the wages of structural iron rivets,
The living lighted skyscrapers tell it now as a name,
Tell it across miles of sea blue water, gray blue land:
I am Chicago, I am a name given out by the breaths of working
    men, laughing men, a child, a belonging.

So between the Great Lakes,
The Grand De Tour, and the Grand Prairie,
The living lighted skyscrapers stand,
Spotting the blue dusk with checkers of yellow,
    streamers of smoke and silver,
    parallelograms of night-gray watchmen,
Singing a soft moaning song: I am a child, a belonging.

    2

How should the wind songs of a windy city go?
Singing in a high wind the dirty chatter gets blown
    away on the wind—the clean shovel,
           the clean pickax,
           lasts.

It is easy for a child to get breakfast and pack off
  to school with a pair of roller skates,
  buns for lunch, and a geography.
Riding through a tunnel under a river running backward,
  to school to listen . . . how the Pottawatomies . . .
  and the Blackhawks . . . ran on moccasins . . .
  between Kaskaskia, Peoria, Kankakee, and Chicago.

It is easy to sit listening to a boy babbling
  of the Pottawatomie moccasins in Illinois,
  how now the roofs and smokestacks cover miles
  where the deerfoot left its writing
  and the foxpaw put its initials
  in the snow . . . for the early moccasins . . . to read.

It is easy for the respectable taxpayers to sit in the
  streetcars and read the papers, faces of burglars,
  the prison escapes, the hunger strikes, the cost of
  living, the price of dying, the shop gate battles of
  strikers and strikebreakers, the strikers killing
  scabs and the police killing strikers—the strongest,
  the strongest, always the strongest.

It is easy to listen to the haberdasher customers hand each other
  their easy chatter—it is easy to die
  alive—to register a living thumbprint and be dead
  from the neck up.
And there are sidewalks polished with the footfalls of
  undertakers' stiffs, greased mannikins, wearing up-to-
  the-minute sox, lifting heels across doorsills,
  shoving their faces ahead of them—dead from the
  neck up—proud of their sox—their sox are the last
  word—dead from the neck up—it is easy.

3

Lash yourself to the bastion of a bridge
and listen while the black cataracts of people go by,
     baggage, bundles, balloons,
     listen while they jazz the classics:

"Since when did you kiss yourself in
And who do you think you are?
Come across, kick in, loosen up.
Where do you get that chatter?"

"Beat up the short-change artists.
They never did nothin' for you.
How do you get that way?
Tell me and I'll tell the world.
I'll say so, I'll say it is."

"You're trying to crab my act.
You poor fish, you mackerel,
You ain't got the sense God
Gave an oyster—it's raining—
What you want is an umbrella."

  "Hush baby—
I don't know a thing.
I don't know a thing.
  Hush baby."

  "Hush baby,
It ain't how old you are,
It's how old you look.
It ain't what you got,
It's what you can get away with."

"Bring home the bacon.
Put it over, shoot it across.
Send 'em to the cleaners.
What we want is results, re-sults
And damn the consequences.
    Sh . . . sh. . . .
You can fix anything
If you got the right fixers."

"Kid each other, you cheap skates.
Tell each other you're all to the mustard—
You're the gravy."

    "Tell 'em, honey.
Ain't it the truth, sweetheart?
    Watch your step.
    You said it.
    You said a mouthful.
We're all a lot of damn fourflushers."

"Hush baby!
    Shoot it,
    Shoot it all!
    Coo coo, coo coo"—
This is one song of Chicago.

4

It is easy to come here a stranger and show the whole works, write
    a book, fix it all up—it is easy to come and go away a muddle-
    headed pig, a bum and a bag of wind.

Go to it and remember this city fished from its
    depths a text: "independent as a hog on ice."

Venice is a dream of soft waters, Vienna and Bagdad recollections of
    dark spears and wild turbans; Paris is a thought in Monet gray
    on scabbards, fabrics, façades; London is a fact in a fog filled with
    the moaning of transatlantic whistles; Berlin sits amid white
    scrubbed quadrangles and torn arithmetics and testaments; Mos-
    cow brandishes a flag and repeats a dance figure of a man who
    walks like a bear.
Chicago fished from its depths a text: Independent
    as a hog on ice.

5

Forgive us if the monotonous houses go mile on mile
Along monotonous streets out to the prairies—
If the faces of the houses mumble hard words
At the streets—and the street voices only say:
"Dust and a bitter wind shall come."
Forgive us if the lumber porches and doorsteps
Snarl at each other—
And the brick chimneys cough in a close-up of
Each other's faces—
And the ramshackle stairways watch each other
As thieves watch—
And dooryard lilacs near a malleable iron works
Long ago languished
In a short whispering purple.

And if the alley ash cans
Tell the garbage-wagon drivers
The children play the alley is Heaven
And the streets of Heaven shine
With a grand dazzle of stones of gold
And there are no policemen in Heaven—
Let the rag-tags have it their way.

And if the geraniums
In the tin cans of the window sills
Ask questions not worth answering—
And if a boy and a girl hunt the sun
With a sieve for sifting smoke—
Let it pass—let the answer be—
"Dust and a bitter wind shall come."

Forgive us if the jazz timebeats
Of these clumsy mass shadows
Moan in saxophone undertones,
And the footsteps of the jungle,
The fang cry, the rip claw hiss,
The sneak-up and the still watch,
The slant of the slit eyes waiting—
If these bother respectable people
       with the right crimp in their napkins
       reading breakfast menu cards—
       forgive us—let it pass—let be.

If cripples sit on their stumps
And joke with the newsies bawling,
"Many lives lost! many lives lost!
Ter-ri-ble ac-ci-dent! many lives lost!"—
If again twelve men let a woman go,
"He done me wrong; I shot him"—
Or the blood of a child's head
Spatters on the hub of a motor truck—
Or a 44-gat cracks and lets the skylights
Into one more bank messenger—
Or if boys steal coal in a railroad yard
And run with humped gunnysacks
While a bull picks off one of the kids
And the kid wriggles with an ear in cinders

And a mother comes to carry home
A bundle, a limp bundle,
To have his face washed, for the last time,
Forgive us if it happens—and happens again—
And happens again.

> Forgive the jazz timebeat
> of clumsy mass shadows,
> footsteps of the jungle,
> the fang cry, the rip claw hiss,
> the slant of the slit eyes waiting.

Forgive us if we work so hard
And the muscles bunch clumsy on us
And we never know why we work so hard—
If the big houses with little families
And the little houses with big families
Sneer at each other's bars of misunderstanding;
Pity us when we shackle and kill each other
And believe at first we understand
And later say we wonder why.

Take home the monotonous patter
Of the elevated railroad guard in the rush hours:
"Watch your step. Watch your step. Watch your step."
Or write on a pocket pad what a pauper said
To a patch of purple asters at a whitewashed wall:
"Let every man be his own Jesus—that's enough."

6

The wheelbarrows grin, the shovels and the mortar
    hoist an exploit.

The stone shanks of the Monadnock, the Transportation,
    the People's Gas Building, stand up and scrape
    at the sky.
The wheelbarrows sing, the bevels and the blueprints
    whisper.
The library building named after Crerar, naked
    as a stock farm silo, light as a single eagle
    feather, stripped like an airplane propeller,
    takes a path up.
Two cool new rivets say, "Maybe it is morning,"
    "God knows."

Put the city up; tear the city down;
    put it up again; let us find a city.
Let us remember the little violet-eyed
    man who gave all, praying, "Dig and
    dream, dream and hammer, till your
    city comes."

Every day the people sleep and the city dies;
    every day the people shake loose, awake and
    build the city again.

The city is a tool chest opened every day,
    a time clock punched every morning,
    a shop door, bunkers and overalls
    counting every day.

The city is a balloon and a bubble plaything
    shot to the sky every evening, whistled in
    a ragtime jig down the sunset.

The city is made, forgotten, and made again,
    trucks hauling it away haul it back

steered by drivers whistling ragtime
against the sunsets.

Every day the people get up and carry the city,
    carry the bunkers and balloons of the city,
    lift it and put it down.

        "I will die as many times
        as you make me over again,
        says the city to the people,
I am the woman, the home, the family,
I get breakfast and pay the rent;
I telephone the doctor, the milkman, the undertaker;
    I fix the streets
    for your first and your last ride—
Come clean with me, come clean or dirty,
I am stone and steel of your sleeping numbers;
    I remember all you forget.
    I will die as many times
    as you make me over again."

Under the foundations,
Over the roofs,
The bevels and the blueprints talk it over.
The wind of the lake shore waits and wanders.
The heave of the shore wind hunches the sand piles.
The winkers of the morning stars count out cities
And forget the numbers.

        7

At the white clock-tower
lighted in night purples
over the boulevard link bridge
only the blind get by without acknowledgments.

The passers-by, factory punch-clock numbers,
    hotel girls out for the air, teameoes,
    coal passers, taxi drivers, window washers,
    paperhangers, floorwalkers, bill collectors,
    burglar alarm salesmen, massage students,
    manicure girls, chiropodists, bath rubbers,
    booze runners, hat cleaners, armhole basters,
    delicatessen clerks, shovel stiffs, work plugs—
They all pass over the bridge, they all look up
    at the white clock-tower
    lighted in night purples
    over the boulevard link bridge—
And sometimes one says, "Well, we hand it to 'em."

Mention proud things, catalogue them.
The jack-knife bridge opening, the ore boats,
    the wheat barges passing through.
Three overland trains arriving the same hour,
    one from Memphis and the cotton belt,
    one from Omaha and the corn belt,
    one from Duluth, the lumberjack and the iron range.
Mention a carload of shorthorns taken off the valleys of Wyoming
    last week, arriving yesterday, knocked in the head, stripped,
    quartered, hung in ice boxes today, mention the daily melodrama
    of this humdrum, rhythms of heads, hides, heels, hoofs hung up.

    8

It is wisdom to think the people are the city.
It is wisdom to think the city would fall to pieces
    and die and be dust in the wind.
If the people of the city all move away and leave no people at all to
    watch and keep the city.

It is wisdom to think no city stood here at all until the working men,
the laughing men, came.
It is wisdom to think tomorrow new working men, new laughing
men, may come and put up a new city—
Living lighted skyscrapers and a night lingo of lanterns testify to-
morrow shall have its own say-so.

9

Night gathers itself into a ball of dark yarn.
Night loosens the ball and it spreads.
The lookouts from the shores of Lake Michigan
    find night follows day, and ping! ping! across
    sheet gray the boat lights put their signals.
Night lets the dark yarn unravel, Night speaks and the yarns change
    to fog and blue strands.

The lookouts turn to the city.
The canyons swarm with red sand lights
    of the sunset.
The atoms drop and sift, blues cross over,
    yellows plunge.
Mixed light shafts stack their bayonets,
    pledge with crossed handles.
So, when the canyons swarm, it is then the
    lookouts speak
Of the high spots over a street . . . mountain language
Of skyscrapers in dusk, the Railway Exchange,
The People's Gas, the Monadnock, the Transportation,
Gone to the gloaming.

The river turns in a half circle.
The Goose Island bridges curve
    over the river curve.

Then the river panorama
performs for the bridge,
dots ... lights ... dots ... lights,
sixes and sevens of dots and lights,
a lingo of lanterns and searchlights,
circling sprays of gray and yellow.

10

A man came as a witness saying:
"I listened to the Great Lakes
And I listened to the Grand Prairie,
And they had little to say to each other,
A whisper or so in a thousand years.
'Some of the cities are big,' said one.
'And some not so big,' said another.
'And sometimes the cities are all gone,'
Said a black knob bluff to a light green sea."

Winds of the Windy City, come out of the prairie,
    all the way from Medicine Hat.
Come out of the inland sea blue water, come where
    they nickname a city for you.

Corn wind in the fall, come off the black lands,
    come off the whisper of the silk hangers,
    the lap of the flat spear leaves.

Blue water wind in summer, come off the blue miles
    of lake, carry your inland sea blue fingers,
    carry us cool, carry your blue to our homes.

White spring winds, come off the bag wool clouds,
    come off the running melted snow, come white
    as the arms of snow-born children.

Gray fighting winter winds, come along on the tear-
    ing blizzard tails, the snouts of the hungry
    hunting storms, come fighting gray in winter.

Winds of the Windy City,
Winds of corn and sea blue,
Spring wind white and fighting winter gray,
Come home here—they nickname a city for you.

The wind of the lake shore waits and wanders.
The heave of the shore wind hunches the sand piles.
The winkers of the morning stars count out cities
And forget the numbers.

❧ IMAGES

[Sandburg] sought what Harriet Monroe described as the "hard clear style" of the Imagists with the elimination of "every unnecessary word, every unstructural ornament."

—PENELOPE NIVEN,
    from *Carl Sandburg: A Biography*

Fog

The fog comes
on little cat feet.

It sits looking
over harbor and city
on silent haunches
and then moves on.

Sketch

The shadows of the ships
Rock on the crest
In the low blue lustre
Of the tardy and the soft inrolling tide.

A long brown bar at the dip of the sky
Puts an arm of sand in the span of salt.

The lucid and endless wrinkles
Draw in, lapse and withdraw.
Wavelets crumble and white spent bubbles
Wash on the floor of the beach.

    Rocking on the crest
    In the low blue lustre
    Are the shadows of the ships.

❧ Lost

Desolate and lone
All night long on the lake
Where fog trails and mist creeps,
The whistle of a boat
Calls and cries unendingly,
Like some lost child
In tears and trouble
Hunting the harbor's breast
And the harbor's eyes.

❧ Flux

Sand of the sea runs red
Where the sunset reaches and quivers.
Sand of the sea runs yellow
Where the moon slants and wavers.

❧ Nocturne in a Deserted Brickyard

Stuff of the moon
Runs on the lapping sand
Out to the longest shadows.

Under the curving willows,
And round the creep of the wave line,
Fluxions of yellow and dusk on the waters
Make a wide dreaming pansy of an old pond in the night.

🌿 *Window*

Night from a railroad car window
Is a great, dark, soft thing
Broken across with slashes of light.

🌿 *Sunset from Omaha Hotel Window*

Into the blue river hills
The red sun runners go
And the long sand changes
And today is a goner
And today is not worth haggling over.

  Here in Omaha
  The gloaming is bitter
  As in Chicago
  Or Kenosha.

The long sand changes.
Today is a goner.
Time knocks in another brass nail.
Another yellow plunger shoots the dark.

Constellations
Wheeling over Omaha
As in Chicago
Or Kenosha.

The long sand is gone
    and all the talk is stars.
They circle in a dome over Nebraska.

🍂 *Prairie Waters by Night*

Chatter of birds two by two raises a night song joining a litany of
    running water—sheer waters showing the russet of old stones
    remembering many rains.

And the long willows drowse on the shoulders of the running water,
    and sleep from much music; joined songs of day-end, feathery
    throats and stony waters, in a choir chanting new psalms.

It is too much for the long willows when low laughter of a red moon
    comes down; and the willows drowse and sleep on the shoulders
    of the running water.

🍂 *Bee Song*

Bees in the late summer sun
Drone their song
Of yellow moons
Trimming black velvet,
Droning, droning a sleepysong.

🐝 Bumble Bee Days

The bumble bees clamber on the saw edges
      of gladiolas.
Lemon-rusty honey bees drone in the ears
      of hollyhocks.
Two leaves of a poplar drift among the
      watching asters.

🐝 Jan Kubelik

Your bow swept over a string, and a long low note quivered to the
    air.
(A mother of Bohemia sobs over a new child perfect learning to suck
    milk.)

Your bow ran fast over all the high strings fluttering and wild.
(All the girls in Bohemia are laughing on a Sunday afternoon in the
    hills with their lovers.)

Chinese Letters or Korean

From a Window

One time the moon whitened the fields, whitened the
    pastures, polished the floor for the dancers;
Let the dancers foot it, earth, legs to the moon,
Look up at the face of the moon and laugh with their
    laughter—
Silver mist, yellow mist, grey mist of dawn,
Eyes open, eyes closing, tell me, did they once lose
    a beat in the measures?—
And let a long brown horse nose to the ground go eating
    tufts of moonshine, go walking from tree
    to proud tree in the ballroom.

· · ·

The moon laughs at these streets.
The tongues of sea mist creep and lick and wind
And say to the trillion lights
A wet night leaves your city—

· · ·

Those who look from a ten story window
Cannot look up at the moon and laugh—
They look out through a lane between bricks over ships,
Widening into a pasture of stars
    above Long Island.
They cannot look up at the moon and laugh.

Their eyes meet the gaze of the moon and catch her high laughter.
"Yes with my gold paint brush I am painting your hotel sky
Immemorial blue, lapis lazuli sky.
But you, though you try and try
May not even touch with your fingers the blue of my sky—
Looking in at your window of bricks
I laugh and laugh again
    Hearing you cry."

❧ *Painted Fishes*

Green fishes on a red-lacquered tray
Are worn bringing a sea of beer
From draught-faucets to oak tables.
Between bartenders and customers
They are losing their green fins.

❧ *These Valleys Seem Old*

(Dedicated to Mrs. Florence Ayscough who lives near Shanghai and whose
translations from inscriptions on Chinese paintings furnished the basis for these
renditions into modern American speech.)

I

The first frost comes now and turns the river water still and clear.
The sky is without a moon. Many stars show.
It is in the valleys near us the watch dogs are barking.
Across the water student lamplights shine.

My forehead burns and then a cold shakes me.
The chills go through my bones. I can hardly stand it.
Thoughts go back and forth about years now gone.
Let us keep off the fishing boats as we go home.

2

In the short grass valleys I lived with hard luck.
I was lonesome and it was no use to talk about it.
Now my wife nags at me to help her with the bamboo shoots for
    winter eating.
My boy is sick; none of his vegetables grow well this year.
About all I will have to live on is mouldy rice.
And dirty wine bought with promises will be about all for drink.
More and more bills are left at my door by tax collectors.
I lean heavy and slow on a stick and go tired to the house of my
    neighbor hoping he will have a little money for me.

3

The water never stops running in the stream at the foot of the
    mountains.
Spring over, green life comes up and shows itself deep between the
    mountains.
On all sides, Force wakes up, young sheep bleat, birds chirp
    learning to fly.
This mulberry thick with leaves was planted by a hand now
    forgotten. Who knows the name of it?

4

The wind blusters; we push off in our boat; we are going to pick
    water chestnuts.

We lean on our sticks and watch the sun set behind the villages to
   the west.
Among the apricot trees we see a fisherman standing with bent
   shoulders; he looks old.
And by the famous Peach Blossom Fountain homes of men stand in
   a cluster.

🌺 *Three Pieces on the Smoke of Autumn*

Smoke of autumn is on it all.
The streamers loosen and travel.
The red west is stopped with a gray haze.
They fill the ash trees, they wrap the oaks,
They make a long-tailed rider
In the pocket of the first, the earliest evening star.

   . . .

Three muskrats swim west on the Desplaines River.

There is a sheet of red ember glow on the river; it is dusk; and the
   muskrats one by one go on patrol routes west.

Around each slippery padding rat, a fan of ripples; in the silence of
   dusk a faint wash of ripples, the padding of the rats going west,
   in a dark and shivering river gold.

(A newspaper in my pocket says the Germans pierce the Italian line;
   I have letters from poets and sculptors in Greenwich Village; I
   have letters from an ambulance man in France and an I. W. W.
   man in Vladivostok.)

I lean on an ash and watch the lights fall, the red ember glow, and
    three muskrats swim west in a fan of ripples on a sheet of river
    gold.

      . . .

Better the blue silence and the gray west,
The autumn mist on the river,
And not any hate and not any love,
And not anything at all of the keen and the deep:

Only the peace of a dog head on a barn floor,
And the new corn shoveled in bushels
And the pumpkins brought from the corn rows,
Umber lights of the dark,
Umber lanterns of the loam dark.

Here a dog head dreams.
Not any hate, not any love.
Not anything but dreams.
Brother of dusk and umber.

POEMS OF PROTEST

Beware of respectable people; beware of crooks, but of all crooks beware *why*
of the respectable; beware of snobs, and especially middle-class snobs; *but his*
beware of people who are perfectly grammatical; beware of culture *Poetry*
hounds; beware of the people who let their thinking be done for them *like this*
and don't know it.

> — CARL SANDBURG, from the *Chicago Daily News*,
>   May 30, 1930

Do tell me how you contrive to be a moral philosopher and a political
agitator at one and the same time—and especially how you contrive to
write such Poets' English one minute and the plain vernacular the next.
The combination is baffling!

> — LILIAN STEICHEN, from *The Poet and the*
>   *Dream Girl: The Love Letters of Lilian Steichen and*
>   *Carl Sandburg*

✿ Billy Sunday

You come along—tearing your shirt—yelling about Jesus. I want
to know what the hell you know about Jesus?

Jesus had a way of talking soft, and everybody except a few
bankers and higher-ups among the con men of Jerusalem liked
to have this Jesus around because he never made any fake
passes, and everything he said went and he helped the sick and
gave the people hope.

You come along squirting words at us, shaking your fist and calling
us all dam fools—so fierce the froth of your own spit slobbers
over your lips—always blabbering we're all going to hell
straight off and you know all about it.

I've read Jesus' words. I know what he said. You don't throw any
scare into me. I've got your number. I know how much you
know about Jesus.

He never came near clean people or dirty people but they felt
cleaner because he came along. It was your crowd of bankers
and business men and lawyers that hired the sluggers and
murderers who put Jesus out of the running.

I say it was the same bunch that's backing you that nailed the nails
into the hands of this Jesus of Nazareth. He had lined up against
him the same crooks and strong-arm men now lined up with
you paying your way.

This Jesus guy was good to look at, smelled good, listened good. He threw out something fresh and beautiful from the skin of his body and the touch of his hands wherever he passed along.

You, Billy Sunday, put a smut on every human blossom that comes in reach of your rotten breath belching about hell-fire and hiccuping about this man who lived a clean life in Galilee.

When are you going to quit making the carpenters build emergency hospitals for women and girls driven crazy with wrecked nerves from your goddam gibberish about Jesus? I put it to you again: What the hell do you know about Jesus?

Go ahead and bust all the chairs you want to. Smash a wagon load of furniture at every performance. Turn sixty somersaults and stand on your nutty head. If it wasn't for the way you scare the women and kids, I'd feel sorry for you and pass the hat.

I like to watch a good four-flusher work, but not when he starts people puking and calling for the doctor.

I like a man that's got guts and can pull off a great, original performance; but you—hell, you're only a bughouse peddler of second-hand gospel—you're only shoving out a phoney imitation of the goods this Jesus guy told us ought to be free as air and sunlight.

Sometimes I wonder what sort of pups born from mongrel bitches there are in the world less heroic, less typic of historic greatness than you.

You tell people living in shanties Jesus is going to fix it up all right with them by giving them mansions in the skies after they're dead and the worms have eaten 'em.

You tell $6 a week department store girls all they need is Jesus; you take a steel trust wop, dead without having lived, gray and shrunken at forty years of age, and you tell him to look at Jesus on the cross and he'll be all right.

You tell poor people they don't need any more money on pay day, and even if it's fierce to be out of a job, Jesus'll fix that all right, all right—all they gotta do is take Jesus the way you say.

I'm telling you this Jesus guy wouldn't stand for the stuff you're handing out. Jesus played it different. The bankers and corporation lawyers of Jerusalem got their sluggers and murderers to go after Jesus just because Jesus wouldn't play their game. He didn't sit in with the big thieves.

I don't want a lot of gab from a bunkshooter in my religion.

I won't take my religion from a man who never works except with his mouth and never cherishes a memory except the face of the woman on the American silver dollar.

I ask you to come through and show me where you're pouring out the blood of your life.

I've been out to this suburb of Jerusalem they call Golgotha, where they nailed Him, and I know if the story is straight it was real blood ran from his hands and the nail-holes, and it was real blood spurted out where the spear of the Roman soldier rammed in between the ribs of this Jesus of Nazareth.

🦅 *The* Eastland

Let's be honest now
For a couple of minutes
Even though we're in Chicago.

Since you ask me about it,
I let you have it straight;
My guts ain't ticklish about the *Eastland*.

It was a hell of a job, of course
To dump 2,500 people in their clean picnic clothes
All ready for a whole lot of real fun
Down into the dirty Chicago river without any warning.

Women and kids, wet hair and scared faces,
The coroner hauling truckloads of the dripping dead
To the Second Regiment armory where doctors waited
With useless pulmotors and the eight hundred motionless stiff
Lay ready for their relatives to pick them out on the floor
And take them home and call up an undertaker . . .

Well I was saying
My guts ain't ticklish about it.
I got imagination: I see a pile of three thousand dead people
Killed by the con,* tuberculosis, too much work
                and not enough fresh air and green groceries

A lot of cheap roughnecks and the women and children of wops,
      and hardly any bankers and corporation lawyers or their kids,

*Consumption.

die from the con—three thousand a year in Chicago and a
hundred and fifty thousand a year in the United States—all
from the con and not enough fresh air and green groceries . . .

If you want to see excitement, more noise and crying than you ever
    heard in one of these big disasters the newsboys clean up on,
Go and stack in a high pile all the babies that die in Christian
    Philadelphia, New York, Boston and Chicago in one year
    because aforesaid babies haven't had enough good milk;
On top the pile put all the little early babies pulled from mothers
    willing to be torn with abortions rather than bring more
    children into the world—
Jesus! that would make a front page picture for the Sunday papers

And you could write under it:
Morning glories
Born from the soil of love,
Yet now perished.

Have you ever stood and watched the kids going to work of a
    morning? White faces, skinny legs and arms, slouching along
    rubbing the sleep out of their eyes on the go to hold their jobs?

Can you imagine a procession of all the whores of a big town,
    marching and marching with painted faces and mocking struts,
    all the women who sleep in faded hotels and furnished rooms
    with any man coming along with a dollar or five dollars?

Or all the structural iron workers, railroad men and factory hands
    in mass formation with stubs of arms and stumps of legs, bodies
    broken and hacked while bosses yelled, "Speed—no slack—
    go to it!"?

Or two by two all the girls and women who go to the hind doors of
    restaurants and through the alleys and on the market street
    digging into the garbage barrels to get scraps of stuff to eat?

By the living Christ, these would make disaster pictures to paste on
the front pages of the newspapers.

Yes, the *Eastland* was a dirty bloody job—bah!
I see a dozen *Eastland*s
Every morning on my way to work
And a dozen more going home at night.

❧ Anna Imroth

Cross the hands over the breast here—so.
Straighten the legs a little more—so.
And call for the wagon to come and take her home.
Her mother will cry some and so will her sisters and brothers.
But all of the others got down and they are safe and this is the only
one of the factory girls who wasn't lucky in making the jump
when the fire broke.
It is the hand of God and the lack of fire escapes.

❧ The Hammer

I have seen
The old gods go
And the new gods come.

Day by day
And year by year
The idols fall
And the idols rise.

Today
I worship the hammer.

1910

Child of the Romans

The dago shovelman sits by the railroad track
Eating a noon meal of bread and bologna.
    A train whirls by, and men and women at tables
    Alive with red roses and yellow jonquils,
    Eat steaks running with brown gravy,
    Strawberries and cream, eclairs and coffee.
The dago shovelman finishes the dry bread and bologna,
Washes it down with a dipper from the water-boy,
And goes back to the second half of a ten-hour day's work
Keeping the road-bed so the roses and jonquils
Shake hardly at all in the cut glass vases
Standing slender on the tables in the dining cars.

Southern Pacific

Huntington sleeps in a house six feet long.
Huntington dreams of railroads he built and owned.
Huntington dreams of ten thousand men saying: Yes, sir.

Blithery sleeps in a house six feet long.
Blithery dreams of rails and ties he laid.
Blithery dreams of saying to Huntington: Yes, sir.

Huntington,
Blithery, sleep in houses six feet long.

🌿 'Boes

I waited today for a freight train to pass.

Cattle cars with steers butting their horns against the bars, went by.

And a half a dozen hoboes stood on bumpers between cars.

Well, the cattle are respectable, I thought.

Every steer has its transportation paid for by the farmer sending it to market,

While the hoboes are law-breakers in riding a railroad train without a ticket.

It reminded me of ten days I spent in the Allegheny County jail in Pittsburgh.

I got ten days even though I was a veteran of the Spanish-American war.

Cooped in the same cell with me was an old man, a bricklayer and a booze-fighter.

But it just happened he, too, was a veteran soldier, and he had fought to preserve the Union and free the niggers.

We were three in all, the other being a Lithuanian who got drunk on payday at the steel works and got to fighting a policeman;

All the clothes he had was a shirt, pants and shoes—somebody got his hat and coat and what money he had left over when he got drunk.

🐝 *Taking on Suds Men Talk*

Taking on suds men talk. One bottle of near-beer
apiece was all Tom and I had. And he told the life
of a woman, his latest hotel find, as she told it to
him. Put short, as no life can be altogether told,
it was like this:

I married a well-off butcher. I didn't love him nor
hate him when I married him and it's the same now as
then. I married him because he went to bed and said
he would never eat again unless I married him. He
starved two days. His mother cried to my mother and
to me. So we went and got a license.

Until he died two years ago, the family doctor used
me when he wanted me. He sent letters saying my health
must not run down. I showed these letters to my husband
and then went to the doctor's office.

A dentist who used me I could never understand. He drilled
one tooth five months and loved me like wild every
time I sat in the big chair and he straightened my knees
and feet on the extensions. Though he went as far as love
could go with me, he always sent bills for services.

Once I was sick three months. I told my mother how I was.
She said it was a baby. I told her it would be terrible to
have a doctor run a knife across my belly. Then my
mother told me there is no knife when a baby is born. She said

"It comes out the same place it goes in." Why did no one tell me this till so late?

The baby came. It was a beautiful baby and strong. Why did it live only two years? I don't know what it died of. Sometimes I think it was afraid of our house, something wrong, and didn't want to grow up with us.

I found out my husband was trying to get a sixteen year old girl neighbor. He was telling me, "If you go with other men I kill you." I made a date with the family doctor that week and kept it.

We have money from the butcher shop. I took piano lessons. I know elocution and recite long poems. And all the time I am hunting more life—nothing satisfies me—what will become of me?

❧ *Glimmer*

Let down your braids of hair, lady.
Cross your legs and sit before the looking-glass
And gaze long on lines under your eyes.
Life writes; men dance.
    And you know how men pay women.

❧ Jerry

Six years I worked in a knitting mill at a machine
And then I married Jerry, the iceman, for a change.
He weighed 240 pounds, and could hold me,
Who weighed 105 pounds, outward easily with one hand.
He came home drunk and lay on me with the breath of stale beer
Blowing from him and jumbled talk that didn't mean anything.
I stood it two years and one hot night when I refused him
And he struck his bare fist against my nose so it bled,
I waited till he slept, took a revolver from a bureau drawer,
Placed the end of it to his head and pulled the trigger.
From the stone walls where I am incarcerated for the natural term
Of life, I proclaim I would do it again.

❧ Horses and Men in Rain

Let us sit by a hissing steam radiator a winter's day, gray wind
    pattering frozen raindrops on the window,
And let us talk about milk wagon drivers and grocery delivery boys.

Let us keep our feet in wool slippers and mix hot punches—and talk
    about mail carriers and messenger boys slipping along the icy
    sidewalks.
Let us write of olden, golden days and hunters of the Holy Grail
    and men called "knights" riding horses in the rain, in the cold
    frozen rain for ladies they loved.

A roustabout hunched on a coal wagon goes by, icicles drip on his
hat rim, sheets of ice wrapping the hunks of coal, the caravanserai
a gray blur in slant of rain.

Let us nudge the steam radiator with our wool slippers and write
poems of Launcelot, the hero, and Roland, the hero, and all the
olden golden men who rode horses in the rain.

✿ Hoodlums

I am a hoodlum, you are a hoodlum, we and all of us are a world of
hoodlums—maybe so.

I hate and kill better men than I am, so do you, so do all of us—
maybe—maybe so.

In the ends of my fingers the itch for another man's neck, I want to
see him hanging, one of dusk's cartoons against the sunset.

This is the hate my father gave me, this was in my mother's milk,
this is you and me and all of us in a world of hoodlums—
maybe so.

Let us go on, brother hoodlums, let us kill and kill, it has always
been so, it will always be so, there is nothing more to it.

Let us go on, sister hoodlums, kill, kill, and kill, the torsos of the
world's mothers are tireless and the loins of the world's fathers
are strong—so go on—kill, kill, kill.

Lay them deep in the dirt, the stiffs we fixed, the cadavers bumped
off, lay them deep and let the night winds of winter blizzards
howl their burial service.

The night winds and the winter, the great white sheets of northern
blizzards, who can sing better for the lost hoodlums the old
requiem, "Kill him! kill him! . . ."

Today my son, tomorrow yours, the day after your next door neighbor's—it is all in the wrists of the gods who shoot craps—it is anybody's guess whose eyes shut next.

Being a hoodlum now, you and I, being all of us a world of hoodlums, let us take up the cry when the mob sluffs by on a thousand shoe soles, let us too yammer, "Kill him! kill him! . . ."

Let us do this now . . . for our mothers . . . for our sisters and wives . . . let us kill, kill, kill—for the torsos of the women are tireless and the loins of the men are strong.

                                        Chicago, July 29, 1919

❧ The Mayor of Gary

I asked the Mayor of Gary about the 12-hour day and the 7-day week.

And the Mayor of Gary answered more workmen steal time on the job in Gary than any other place in the United States.

"Go into the plants and you will see men sitting around doing nothing—machinery does everything," said the Mayor of Gary when I asked him about the 12-hour day and the 7-day week.

And he wore cool cream pants, the Mayor of Gary, and white shoes, and a barber had fixed him up with a shampoo and a shave and he was easy and imperturbable though the government weather bureau thermometer said 96 and children were soaking their heads at bubbling fountains on the street corners.

And I said good-by to the Mayor of Gary and I went out from the city hall and turned the corner into Broadway.

And I saw workmen wearing leather shoes scruffed with fire and cinders, and pitted with little holes from running molten steel,

And some had bunches of specialized muscles around their shoulder
    blades hard as pig iron, muscles of their forearms were sheet steel
    and they looked to me like men who had been somewhere.

Gary, Indiana, 1915

❧ Blacklisted

Why shall I keep the old name?
What is a name anywhere anyway?
A name is a cheap thing all fathers and mothers leave each child:
A job is a job and I want to live, so
Why does God Almighty or anybody else care whether I take a new
    name to go by?

❧ The Machine

    The machine yes the machine
    never wastes anybody's time
    never watches the foreman
    never talks back
    never talks what is right or wrong
    never listens to others talking or if
        it does listen it doesn't hear
    never says we've been thinking, or, our
        feeling is like this
the machine yes the machine cuts your production cost
a man is a man and what can you do with him?
but a machine now you take a machine

no kids   no woman   never hungry   never thirsty
all a machine needs is a little regular attention and plenty
    of grease.

🐦 *Legal Midnight Hour*

Well, the dying time came, the legal midnight hour,
The moment set by law for the Chair to be at work,
To substantiate the majesty of the State of Massachusetts
That hour was at hand, had arrived, was struck by the clocks,
The time for two men to be carried cool on a cooling board
Beyond the immeasurably thin walls between day and night,
Beyond the reach of airmail, telegrams, radiophones,
Beyond the brotherhoods of blood into the fraternities
Of mist and foggy dew, of stars and ice.
    The time was on for two men
    To march beyond blood into dust—
    A time that comes to all men,
    Some with a few loved ones at a bedside,
    Some alone in the wilderness or the wide sea,
    Some before a vast audience of all mankind.

    Now Sacco saw the witnesses
    As the straps were fitted on
    Tying him down in the Chair—
    And seeing the witnesses were
Respectable men and responsible citizens
And even though there had been no introductions,
    Sacco said, "Good-evening, gentlemen."
And before the last of the straps was fastened so to hold
Sacco murmured, "Farewell, mother."

Then came Vanzetti.
He wished the vast audience of all mankind
To know something he carried in his breast.
This was the time to tell it.
He had to speak now or hold his peace forever.
The headgear was being clamped on.
The straps muffling his mouth were going on.
He shouted, "I wish to forgive some people
          for what they are now doing."
     And so now
     the dead are dead? ? ? ?

❧ LOVE POEMS

Love, is it a cat with claws and wild mate screams in the black night?
Love, l-o-v-e, is it a tug at the heart that comes high and costs, always
  costs, as long as you have it?
Love, is it a free glad spender, ready to spend to the limit and then go
  head over heels in debt?
Love, can it hit one without hitting two, and leave the one lost and
  groping?

  —CARL SANDBURG, from *The World*
    of Carl Sandburg

❧ *Paula*

Nothing else in this song—only your face.
Nothing else here—only your drinking, night-gray eyes.

The pier runs into the lake straight as a rifle barrel.
I stand on the pier and sing how I know you mornings.
It is not your eyes, your face, I remember.
It is not your dancing, race-horse feet.
It is something else I remember you for on the pier mornings.

Your hands are sweeter than nut-brown bread when you touch me.
Your shoulder brushes my arm—a south-west wind crosses the
    pier.
I forget your hands and your shoulder and I say again:

Nothing else in this song—only your face.
Nothing else here—only your drinking, night-gray eyes.

❧ *White Shoulders*

Your white shoulders
    I remember
And your shrug of laughter.

    Low laughter
    Shaken slow
From your white shoulders.

June

Paula is digging and shaping the loam of a salvia,
    Scarlet Chinese talker of summer.
Two petals of crabapple blossom blow fallen in Paula's hair,
    And fluff of white from a cottonwood.

Poppies

She loves blood-red poppies for a garden to walk in.
In a loose white gown she walks
               and a new child tugs at cords in her body.
Her head to the west at evening when the dew is creeping,
A shudder of gladness runs in her bones and torsal fiber:
She loves blood-red poppies for a garden to walk in.

Margaret

Many birds and the beating of wings
Make a flinging reckless hum
In the early morning at the rocks
Above the blue pool
Where the gray shadows swim lazy.

In your blue eyes, O reckless child,
I saw today many little wild wishes,
Eager as the great morning.

Baby Toes

There is a blue star, Janet,
Fifteen years' ride from us,
If we ride a hundred miles an hour.

There is a white star, Janet,
Forty years' ride from us,
If we ride a hundred miles an hour.

Helga

The wishes on this child's mouth
Came like snow on marsh cranberries;
The tamarack kept something for her;
The wind is ready to help her shoes.
The north has loved her; she will be
A grandmother feeding geese on frosty
Mornings; she will understand
Early snow on the cranberries
Better and better then.

❧ Spanish

Fasten black eyes on me.
I ask nothing of you under the peach trees,
Fasten your black eyes in my gray
            with the spear of a storm.
The air under the peach blossoms is a haze of pink.

❧ You and a Sickle Moon

The lips of you are with me tonight.
And the arms of you are a circle of white.

The dream of it burns.
And I want you and the stars.
I want you and a sickle moon.

The finger tips of you
Five hundred miles away
Make a wireless crying flash:
I know a search that's useless,
I know a code I don't hunt for,
I know a face that's gone.

Back home the hills talk to me.
Here the hills are strangers.

The lips of you are a ghost.
The arms of you are a ghost.
    The red and white is empty air.

Omaha 1917

🌑 *In Blue Gown and in Black Satin Gown*

she wore a blue gown for him once
the fabric flowing with her curves
only the hair of long black eyelashes
flashing naked for his eyes:
a mist of wanting gathered
a black-ice loneliness between them:
    she loosened the blue gown
    and lay bare before him
        a smooth miracle of dawn
        a silent shingle of lights—
            so they hid themselves
            in a winding sheet of passion
            in a little hut of shaken walls

she wore a black satin gown for him once
the flow of her hips a poem of night
moving in a dusk of her long eyelashes
    standing they held a greeting kiss
    murmured of the ritual to come
        she lay waiting for him
        lifting the black satin
        gleaming over a white navel
            she drew him in with familiar sheaths
            they lay in a room of blood-rose shadows

hearing many clocks in a music of bronze
in flesh tones of a cool vesper twilight
   slowly they moved into storm and drums
   into a whirl of changing light-spokes
      her white torso lost in satin shadows
      sank in a moan of white blossoms
      in a falling sheen of black moonlight.

❧ *She Held Herself a Deep Pool for Him*

she held herself a deep pool for him
and the shadows crying for him
he gathered himself in many dark waters
and the shadows crying for her
they took each other in shadow meetings
they held themselves in shadow songs

   she coiled herself around him
   with a ribbon of glass
   and a rope of gold
   the coils of her cunning held him
   with rings of golden glass
   with a moon of melting gold
   with a mist of sunset ribbons

🐝 An Interwoven Man and Woman Talked

An interwoven man and woman talked.
The mesh of a red rose held the man.
A moist evening dew beheld the two.
Their speech was in even vocabularies.
Their voices comprised several violins.
The lights of changing weather were there.
They talked of kingdoms, empires, republics.
They spoke of mice, dice, republicans, democrats,
How stars may be foiled of grand desires,
How love may be wept over as an abstraction,
How black velvet may suddenly transfuse
With tracks and spatters of red blood,
How fate waits at a door with a white finger,
How beautiful children become drab vagabonds,
How the coin of life comes willy-nilly,
How Jesus was not ashamed of miracles.

🐝 Troth Tryst

There is a troth between us.
A troth means we are to keep
a tryst.

A tryst means we shall drop into
a dappled sea together.
The sea is a grand smooth clamor,
bitter with fish, drowsy with dream
blossoms.

🌸 *Offering and Rebuff*

I could love you
as dry roots love rain.
I could hold you
as branches in the wind
brandish petals.
Forgive me for speaking
so soon.

. . .

Let your heart look
on white sea spray
and be lonely.

Love is a fool star.

You and a ring of stars
may mention my name
and then forget me.

Love is a fool star.

. . .

❧ Hellcat

He had arguments about a woman.
He argued to himself about her.
She was a hellcat, he argued.
Crazy, never the same two minutes.
Yet her breasts were hills of passion,
Her tongue made for swift kissing,
Her torso holding sanctuaries
Strange as the lost temples
Of sunken archipelagoes—
She carried sacraments for him
Yet his words for her were hellcat,
Crazy woman.

❧ Bilbea

(From tablet writing, Babylonian excavations of 4th millennium B.C.)

Bilbea, I was in Babylon on Saturday night.
I saw nothing of you anywhere.
I was at the old place and the other girls were there, but no Bilbea.

Have you gone to another house? or city?
Why don't you write?
I was sorry. I walked home half-sick.

Tell me how it goes.
Send me some kind of a letter.
And take care of yourself.

✿ LINCOLN

Not often in the story of mankind does a man arrive on earth who is both steel and velvet, who is hard as a rock and soft as a drifting fog, who holds in his heart and mind the paradox of terrible storm and peace unspeakable and perfect.

— CARL SANDBURG, from his Lincoln address at a Joint Session of Congress, February 12, 1959

🌺 Fire-Logs

Nancy Hanks dreams by the fire;
Dreams, and the logs sputter,
And the yellow tongues climb.
Red lines lick their way in flickers.
Oh, sputter, logs.
      Oh, dream, Nancy.
Time now for a beautiful child.
Time now for a tall man to come.

🌺 In a Back Alley

Remembrance for a great man is this.
The newsies are pitching pennies.
And on the copper disk is the man's face.
Dead lover of boys, what do you ask for now?

🌺 Knucks

In Abraham Lincoln's city,
Where they remember his lawyer's shingle,
The place where they brought him
Wrapped in battle flags,

Wrapped in the smoke of memories
From Tallahassee to the Yukon,
The place now where the shaft of his tomb
Points white against the blue prairie dome,
In Abraham Lincoln's city . . . I saw knucks
In the window of Mister Fischman's second-hand store
On Second Street.

I went in and asked, "How much?"
"Thirty cents apiece," answered Mister Fischman.
And taking a box of new ones off a shelf
He filled anew the box in the showcase
And said incidentally, most casually
And incidentally:
"I sell a carload a month of these."

I slipped my fingers into a set of knucks,
Cast-iron knucks molded in a foundry pattern,
And there came to me a set of thoughts like these:
Mister Fischman is for Abe and the "malice to none" stuff,
And the street car strikers and the strike-breakers,
And the sluggers, gunmen, detectives, policemen,
Judges, utility heads, newspapers, priests, lawyers,
They are all for Abe and the "malice to none" stuff.

I started for the door.
"Maybe you want a lighter pair,"
Came Mister Fischman's voice.
I opened the door . . . and the voice again:
"You are a funny customer."

Wrapped in battle flags,
Wrapped in the smoke of memories,
This is the place they brought him,
This is Abraham Lincoln's home town.

❧ The People, Yes

57

Lincoln?
He was a mystery in smoke and flags
saying yes to the smoke, yes to the flags,
yes to the paradoxes of democracy,
yes to the hopes of government
of the people by the people for the people,
no to debauchery of the public mind,
no to personal malice nursed and fed,
yes to the Constitution when a help,
no to the Constitution when a hindrance,
yes to man as a struggler amid illusions,
each man fated to answer for himself:
Which of the faiths and illusions of mankind
must I choose for my own sustaining light
to bring me beyond the present wilderness?

    Lincoln? was he a poet?
    and did he write verses?
"I have not willingly planted a thorn
    in any man's bosom."
"I shall do nothing through malice; what
    I deal with is too vast for malice."

Death was in the air.
So was birth.

What was dying few could say.
What was being born none could know.

He took the wheel in a lashing roaring
   hurricane.
And by what compass did he steer the course
   of the ship?
"My policy is to have no policy," he said in
   the early months,
And three years later, "I have been controlled
   by events."

He could play with the wayward human mind, saying at Charleston,
   Illinois, September 18, 1858, it was no answer to an argument to
   call a man a liar.
"I assert that you [pointing a finger in the face of a man in the
   crowd] are here today, and you undertake to prove me a liar by
   showing that you were in Mattoon yesterday.
"I say that you took your hat off your head and you prove me a liar
   by putting it on your head."

   He saw personal liberty across wide horizons.
"Our progress in degeneracy appears to me to be pretty rapid," he
   wrote Joshua F. Speed, August 24, 1855. "As a nation we began
   by declaring that 'all men are created equal, except negroes.'
   When the Know-Nothings get control, it will read 'all men are
   created equal except negroes and foreigners and Catholics.'
   When it comes to this, I shall prefer emigrating to some country
   where they make no pretense of loving liberty."

   Did he look deep into a crazy pool
   and see the strife and wrangling
   with a clear eye, writing the military
   head of a stormswept area:
   "If both factions, or neither, shall abuse

you, you will probably be about right.
Beware of being assailed by one and
praised by the other"?

Lincoln? was he a historian?
did he know mass chaos?
did he have an answer for those
who asked him to organize chaos?

"Actual war coming, blood grows hot, and blood is spilled. Thought
is forced from old channels into confusion. Deception breeds and
thrives. Confidence dies and universal suspicion reigns.

"Each man feels an impulse to kill his neighbor, lest he be first killed
by him. Revenge and retaliation follow. And all this, as before
said, may be among honest men only; but this is not all.

"Every foul bird comes abroad and every dirty reptile rises up.
These add crime to confusion.

"Strong measures, deemed indispensable, but harsh at best, such men
make worse by maladministration. Murders for old grudges, and
murders for pelf, proceed under any cloak that will best cover for
the occasion. These causes amply account for what has happened
in Missouri."

Early in '64 the Committee of the New York Workingman's Dem-
ocratic Republican Association called on him with assurances and
he meditated aloud for them, recalling race and draft riots:

"The most notable feature of a disturbance in your city last
summer was the hanging of some working people by other
working people. It should never be so.

"The strongest bond of human sympathy, outside of the family
relation, should be one uniting all working people, of all
nations and tongues and kindreds.

"Let not him who is houseless pull down the house of another,
but let him labor diligently and build one for himself, thus by

example assuring that his own shall be safe from violence
when built."

Lincoln? did he gather
the feel of the American dream
and see its kindred over the earth?

"As labor is the common burden of our race,
so the effort of some to shift
their share of the burden
onto the shoulders of others
is the great durable curse of the race."

"I hold,
if the Almighty had ever made a set of men
that should do all of the eating
and none of the work,
he would have made them
with mouths only, and no hands;
and if he had ever made another class,
that he had intended should do all the work
and none of the eating,
he would have made them
without mouths and all hands."

"—the same spirit that says, 'You toil and
work and earn bread, and I'll eat it.' No
matter in what shape it comes, whether
from the mouth of a king who seeks to
bestride the people of his own nation
and live by the fruit of their labor, or
from one race of men as an apology for
enslaving another race, it is the same
tyrannical principle."

"As I would not be a slave, so I would not
     be a master. This expresses my idea of
     democracy. Whatever differs from this,
     to the extent of the difference, is no de-
     mocracy."

"I never knew a man who wished to be him-
     self a slave. Consider if you know any
     good thing that no man desires for him-
     self."

"The sheep and the wolf
     are not agreed upon a definition
     of the word liberty."

"The whole people of this nation
     will ever do well
     if well done by."

"The plainest print cannot be read
through a gold eagle."

"How does it feel to be President?" an
     Illinois friend asked.

"Well, I'm like the man they rode out of
     town on a rail. He said if it wasn't for
     the honor of it he would just as soon
     walk."

          Lincoln? he was a dreamer.
          He saw ships at sea,
          he saw himself living and dead
          in dreams that came.

Into a secretary's diary December 23, 1863
     went an entry: "The President tonight

had a dream. He was in a party of plain
people, and, as it became known who
he was, they began to comment on his
appearance. One of them said: 'He is a
very common-looking man.' The Presi-
dent replied: 'The Lord prefers com-
mon-looking people. That is the reason
he makes so many of them.'"

He spoke one verse for then and now:
"If we could first know where we are,
and whither we are tending,
we could better judge
what to do, and how to do it."

🌿 *The Long Shadow of Lincoln: A Litany*

(We can succeed only by concert. . . . The dogmas of the quiet past are
inadequate to the stormy present. The occasion is piled high with difficulty,
and we must rise with the occasion. As our case is new so we must think anew
and act anew. We must disenthrall ourselves. . . . December 1, 1862. *The
President's Message to Congress.*)

Be sad, be cool, be kind,
remembering those now dreamdust
hallowed in the ruts and gullies,
solemn bones under the smooth blue sea,
faces warblown in a falling rain.

Be a brother, if so can be,
to those beyond battle fatigue
each in his own corner of earth

or forty fathoms undersea
beyond all boom of guns,
beyond any bong of a great bell,
each with a bosom and number,
each with a pack of secrets,
each with a personal dream and doorway
and over them now the long endless winds
with the low healing song of time,
the hush and sleep murmur of time.

Make your wit a guard and cover.
Sing low, sing high, sing wide.
Let your laughter come free
remembering looking toward peace:
"We must disenthrall ourselves."

Be a brother, if so can be,
to those thrown forward
for taking hardwon lines,
for holding hardwon points
and their reward so-so,
little they care to talk about,
their pay held in a mute calm,
highspot memories going unspoken,
what they did being past words,
what they took being hardwon.
Be sad, be kind, be cool.
Weep if you must
And weep open and shameless
before these altars.

There are wounds past words.
There are cripples less broken
than many who walk whole.

There are dead youths
with wrists of silence
who keep a vast music
under their shut lips,
what they did being past words,
their dreams like their deaths
beyond any smooth and easy telling,
having given till no more to give.

There is dust alive
with dreams of The Republic,
with dreams of the Family of Man
flung wide on a shrinking globe
with old timetables,
old maps, old guide-posts
torn into shreds,
shot into tatters,
burnt in a firewind,
lost in the shambles,
faded in rubble and ashes.

There is dust alive.
Out of a granite tomb,
Out of a bronze sarcophagus,
Loose from the stone and copper
Steps a whitesmoke ghost
Lifting an authoritative hand
In the name of dreams worth dying for,
In the name of men whose dust breathes
of those dreams so worth dying for,
what they did being past words,
beyond all smooth and easy telling.

Be sad, be kind, be cool,
remembering, under God, a dreamdust
hallowed in the ruts and gullies,
solemn bones under the smooth blue sea,
faces warblown in a falling rain.

Sing low, sing high, sing wide.
Make your wit a guard and cover.
Let your laughter come free
like a help and a brace of comfort.

The earth laughs, the sun laughs
over every wise harvest of man,
over man looking toward peace
by the light of the hard old teaching:
    "We must disenthrall ourselves."

Read as the Phi Beta Kappa poem at the Mother Chapter of William and Mary College, Williamsburg, Virginia, December, 1944. Published in the *Saturday Evening Post*, February, 1945.

❧ *Abraham Lincoln's Father and Mother**

Who was Abraham Lincoln's father?
Who was Abraham Lincoln's mother?
These are questions.
And a question seems to be a way of saying, "I don't know—can
    you tell me?"
Or a question is a way of saying, "I know a little or I know much
    about something—can you tell me more about it?"

*Previously unpublished

Or it is a way of saying, "I know enough and a plenty to satisfy me—yet there is the tragic or comic in the scrolls people unroll in answers."

Or a question says, "Must we not have something to talk about? Were not tongues given us to be slipping words from? Is not the asking and answering of questions a way of passing the time while half alive for those who find that silence hurts and songs will not come?"

So . . . there are two questions . . . who was the man whose loins fathered Abe Lincoln? . . . who was the woman whose tissues held him and gave him into the world of dark red life he lived?

These are questions.

If the sheets of the seed planting that grew him, were under a lawful and ordered roof—

Or, if the earliest spring night of his life was in a drifting rain drizzle under a black oak tree or a white ash—

If he came under the speech of solemn and understood oaths where there was a door, a fire and a chimney—

Or if he came with only hills and stars for witnesses, with leaves and night wind whispering—

By either way or time there may be questions, there may be answers.

Who was Abe Lincoln's father? . . . Mother?

I don't know—can you tell me?

I know a little—can you tell me more?

I know enough to satisfy me.

1914

🌿 Lincoln*

Beat against the wall, O shadows.
Gateways are called for.
Open the valley doors.
It is night and loons sit chattering.
It is night and hyenas rip the guts of babies.
It is night and the drinkers of blood are too many.
It is night and the yawling of jungle breeds goes on.
Beat against the wall, O shadows,
The backwashes of hurricanes rise, move on and call for
    their toll of the strangler's meshes.
Open the gateways, the valley doors.
Sit with your hands the same as always.
Baboon face, keep on sitting still.
Muttering, mumbling baboon, sit still.
Singing baboon, it is such a low song you sing to yourself.
Yah-yah, loo-loo, it is such a low song beating against the
    wall, the shadows, praying for the gateway, the valley
    doors—yah-yah, loo-loo.
Sit with your hands the same as always.

1915

*Previously unpublished

🌺 *Mr. Lincoln and His Gloves**

Mr. Lincoln on his way to Washington
to be the President of the United States
stays in New York City two days
and one night goes to the Opera.
Sits in a box, his lean speaking hands
    on a red velvet railing.
And the audience notices something.
Yes, notices.
Mr. Lincoln is wearing gloves
        kid gloves
        black kid gloves.

The style
the vogue
the fashion is white kid gloves.
On the main floor
in the balcony
in the boxes
the gloves are correct and white.

A gentleman in another box tells his ladies:
"I think we ought to send some flowers over the way
to the Undertaker of the Union."

Soon we see Mr. Lincoln in Washington kissing the Bible
swearing to be true to the Constitution.

*Posthumously published

Lincoln holding in his heart these words:
"I have not willingly planted a thorn in any man's bosom.
I shall do nothing through malice.
What I deal with is too vast for malice."

Now we see Mr. Lincoln at a White House reception
His fingers swollen, his white gloves
    twisted by a mob of handshakes.
His right hand at last giving an extra strong handshake
to an Illinois man, an Illinois man he knew long ago.
Then it happens!
His right glove cracks and goes to pieces.
He holds his hand up, looks at the dangling glove.
"Well, my old friend, this is a general bustification,
you and I were never meant to wear these things."

Another time, Mr. Lincoln rides away in a White House
    carriage.
Next to him an old western friend, wearing brand new
        white kid gloves.
Mr. Lincoln notices, can't help noticing those brand
    new white tight gloves.
Mr. Lincoln digs down into his pocket.
Feels around and brings out his own brand new white
    kid gloves,
begins squeezing his fingers and thumbs in
when the old friend cries:
"No, no, Mr. Lincoln,
put up your gloves, Mr. Lincoln."
And they ride along, talk and joke, no more bother,
                    sitting pretty
                    sitting easy
                    as two old worn gloves.

Often Mr. Lincoln cannot find his gloves.
Sometimes Mr. Lincoln forgets his gloves.
Often Mrs. Lincoln gives him a new pair, a nice, correct
fashionable pair of gloves.

And one day a California newspaper man
sees him hunting in his overcoat pocket
for a pair of gloves.
Bringing out one pair
he digs deeper
and brings out another pair.
Then into another pocket.
Out comes

        three
        four
        five
        six
        seven
        more pairs of gloves.

That was one time
if Mr. Lincoln had anything plenty of
it was gloves.

You and I may be sure Mr. Lincoln never in his life
felt sorry for himself about his gloves.

When he forgot his gloves
maybe he was too deep with remembering
men fighting, men dying, on consecrated ground.
Too deep with remembering
his hope
"Government of the people
by the people

for the people
shall not perish from the earth."

And there is no good reason why you,
                    why I,
                    why we
            should ever worry
about Mr. Lincoln and his gloves.

🌺 *Journey and Oath**

When Abraham Lincoln received a bullet in the head
    and was taken to the Peterson house across the
    street,
He passed on and was swathed in emulsions and pre-
    pared for a journey to New York, Niagara, across
    Ohio, Indiana, back to Illinois—

As he lay looking life-like yet not saying a word,
Lay portentous and silent under a glass cover,
Lay with oracular lips still as a winter leaf,
Lay deaf to the drums of regiments coming and going,
Lay blind to the weaving causes of work or war or peace,
Lay as an inextinguishable symbol of toil, thought, sacrifice—

There was an oath in the heart of this man and that:
        By God, I'll go as a Man;
        When my time comes I'll be ready.
        I shall keep the faith that nothing
            is impossible with man, that one
            or two illusions are good as money.

*Posthumously published

By God, I'll be true to Man
As against hog, louse, fox, snake, wolf,
As against these and their counterparts
   in the breast of Man.
By God, I'll fight for Man
As against famine, flood, storm,
As against crop gambling, job gambling,
As against bootlickers on the left hand,
As against bloodsuckers on the right hand,
As against the cannibalism of the exploitation
   of man by man,
As against insecurity of the sanctities of
   human life.

1915

🌿 *Untitled**

Paint his head against lavender shadows.
Fling stars around howsoever you choose.
The wing tips of birds circling sunset
Arches of measureless fading gates.
Put in mystery without end.
This man was mystery.
And yet at the end of your hands technique
Of fixing mystery around a head,
Let up on the mystery. Mix in among the
Lavender shadows the gorilla far back
And the jungle cry of readiness for death
Or struggle—and the clean breeds who live on
In the underbrush. Mix in farther back yet

*Previously unpublished

Breeds out of the slime of the sea.
Put in a high green of a restless sea.
Insinuate chlorine and mystic salts,
The make-up of vertebrates,
The long highway of mammals who chew
Their victims and feed their children
From milk at a breast. Let him cry from silence
How the fathers and the women went hungry
And battled hunger and tore each other's jugulars
Over land and women, laughter and language.
Put in mystery without end. Then add mystery.

ANTI-WAR AND
WAR POEMS

*Millions of men go to war, acres of them are buried, guns and ships
broken, cities burned, villages sent up in smoke, and children where
cows are killed off amid hoarse barbecues vanish like finger-rings of
smoke in a north wind.*

— CARL SANDBURG, from "Smoke,"
in *Complete Poems*

✀ House

Two Swede families live downstairs and an Irish policeman upstairs, and an old soldier, Uncle Joe.

Two Swede boys go upstairs and see Joe. His wife is dead, his only son is dead, and his two daughters in Missouri and Texas don't want him around.

The boys and Uncle Joe crack walnuts with a hammer on the bottom of a flatiron while the January wind howls and the zero air weaves laces on the window glass.

Joe tells the Swede boys all about Chickamauga and Chattanooga, how the Union soldiers crept in rain somewhere a dark night and ran forward and killed many Rebels, took flags, held a hill, and won a victory told about in the histories in school.

Joe takes a piece of carpenter's chalk, draws lines on the floor and piles stove wood to show where six regiments were slaughtered climbing a slope.

"Here they went" and "Here they went," says Joe, and the January wind howls and the zero air weaves laces on the window glass.

The two Swede boys go downstairs with a big blur of guns, men, and hills in their heads. They eat herring and potatoes and tell the family war is a wonder and soldiers are a wonder.

One breaks out with a cry at supper: I wish we had a war now and I could be a soldier.

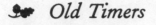 *Old Timers*

I am an ancient reluctant conscript.

On the soup wagons of Xerxes I was a cleaner of pans.

On the march of Miltiades' phalanx I had a haft and head;
I had a bristling gleaming spear-handle.

Red-headed Cæsar picked me for a teamster.
He said, "Go to work, you Tuscan bastard,
Rome calls for a man who can drive horses."

The units of conquest led by Charles the Twelfth,
The whirling whimsical Napoleonic columns:
They saw me one of the horseshoers.

I trimmed the feet of a white horse Bonaparte swept the night stars
    with.

Lincoln said, "Get into the game; your nation takes you."
And I drove a wagon and team and I had my arm shot off
At Spotsylvania Court House.

I am an ancient reluctant conscript.

🐝 *Ready to Kill*

Ten minutes now I have been looking at this.
I have gone by here before and wondered about it.
This is a bronze memorial of a famous general
Riding horseback with a flag and a sword and a revolver on him.
I want to smash the whole thing into a pile of junk to be hauled
    away to the scrap yard.
I put it straight to you,
After the farmer, the miner, the shop man, the factory hand, the
    fireman and the teamster,
Have all been remembered with bronze memorials,
Shaping them on the job of getting all of us
Something to eat and something to wear,
When they stack a few silhouettes
    Against the sky
    Here in the park,
And show the real huskies that are doing the work of the world, and
    feeding people instead of butchering them,
Then maybe I will stand here
And look easy at this general of the army holding a flag in the air,
And riding like hell on horseback
Ready to kill anybody that gets in his way,
Ready to run the red blood and slush the bowels of men all over the
    sweet new grass of the prairie.

🌿 Killers

I am singing to you
Soft as a man with a dead child speaks;
Hard as a man in handcuffs,
Held where he cannot move:

Under the sun
Are sixteen million men,
Chosen for shining teeth,
Sharp eyes, hard legs,
And a running of young warm blood in their wrists.

And a red juice runs on the green grass;
And a red juice soaks the dark soil.
And the sixteen million are killing . . . and killing and killing.

I never forget them day or night:
They beat on my head for memory of them;
They pound on my heart and I cry back to them,
To their homes and women, dreams and games.

I wake in the night and smell the trenches,
And hear the low stir of sleepers in lines—
Sixteen million sleepers and pickets in the dark:
Some of them long sleepers for always,
Some of them tumbling to sleep tomorrow for always,
Fixed in the drag of the world's heartbreak,
Eating and drinking, toiling . . . on a long job of killing.
Sixteen million men.

❧ Planked Whitefish

("I'm agoing to live anyhow until I die."—Modern Ragtime Song)

Over an order of planked whitefish at a downtown club,
Horace Wild, the demon driver who hurled the first aeroplane
   that ever crossed the air over Chicago,
Told Charley Cutler, the famous rassler who never touches
   booze,
And Carl Sandburg, the distinguished poet now out of jail,
He saw near Ypres a Canadian soldier fastened on a barn door
   with bayonets pinning the hands and feet
And the arms and ankles arranged like Jesus at Golgotha 2,000
   years before
Only in northern France he saw
The genital organ of the victim amputated and placed between
   the lips of the dead man's mouth,
And Horace Wild, eating whitefish, looked us straight in the
   eyes,
And piled up circumstantial detail of what he saw one night
   running a truck pulling ambulances out of the mud near
   Ypres in November, 1915:
A box car next to a field hospital operating room . . . filled
   with sawed-off arms and legs . . .
Faces in the gray and the dark on the mud flats, white faces
   gibbering and loose convulsive arms making useless gestures,
And Horace Wild, the demon driver who loves fighting and can
   whip his weight in wildcats,

Pointed at a blue button in the lapel of his coat, "P-e-a-c-e"
    spelled in white letters, and he blurted:
"I don't care who the hell calls me a pacifist. I don't care who
    the hell calls me yellow. I say war is the game of a lot of
    God-damned fools."

🌺 *Murmurings in a Field Hospital*

(They picked him up in the grass where he had lain two days in the rain with a
piece of shrapnel in his lungs.)

Come to me only with playthings now . . .
A picture of a singing woman with blue eyes
Standing at a fence of hollyhocks, poppies and sunflowers . . .
Or an old man I remember sitting with children telling stories
Of days that never happened anywhere in the world . . .

No more iron cold and real to handle,
Shaped for a drive straight ahead.
Bring me only beautiful useless things.
Only old home things touched at sunset in the quiet . . .
And at the window one day in summer
Yellow of the new crock of butter
Stood against the red of new climbing roses . . .
And the world was all playthings.

Buttons

I have been watching the war map slammed up for advertising in front of the newspaper office.
Buttons—red and yellow buttons—blue and black buttons—are shoved back and forth across the map.

A laughing young man, sunny with freckles,
Climbs a ladder, yells a joke to somebody in the crowd,
And then fixes a yellow button one inch west
And follows the yellow button with a black button one inch west.

(Ten thousand men and boys twist on their bodies in a red soak along a river edge,
Gasping of wounds, calling for water, some rattling death in their throats.)
Who would guess what it cost to move two buttons one inch on the war map here in front of the newspaper office where the freckle-faced young man is laughing to us?

Salvage

Guns on the battle lines have pounded now a year between Brussels and Paris.
And, William Morris, when I read your old chapter on the great arches and naves and little whimsical corners of the Churches of Northern France—Brr-rr!

I'm glad you're a dead man, William Morris, I'm glad you're down
    in the damp and mouldy, only a memory instead of a living
    man—I'm glad you're gone.
You never lied to us, William Morris, you loved the shape of those
    stones piled and carved for you to dream over and wonder be-
    cause workmen got joy of life into them,
Workmen in aprons singing while they hammered, and praying, and
    putting their songs and prayers into the walls and roofs, the
    bastions and cornerstones and gargoyles—all their children and
    kisses of women and wheat and roses growing.
I say, William Morris, I'm glad you're gone, I'm glad you're a dead
    man.
Guns on the battle lines have pounded a year now between Brussels
    and Paris.

Wars

In the old wars drum of hoofs and the beat of shod feet.
In the new wars hum of motors and the tread of rubber tires.
In the wars to come silent wheels and whirr of rods not yet dreamed
    out in the heads of men.

In the old wars clutches of short swords and jabs into faces with
    spears.
In the new wars long-range guns and smashed walls, guns running a
    spit of metal and men falling in tens and twenties.
In the wars to come new silent deaths, new silent hurlers not yet
    dreamed out in the heads of men.

In the old wars kings quarreling and thousands of men following.
In the new wars kings quarreling and millions of men following.

In the wars to come kings kicked under the dust and millions of men following great causes not yet dreamed out in the heads of men.

❧ A Million Young Workmen, 1915

A million young workmen straight and strong lay stiff on the grass and roads,

And the million are now under soil and their rottening flesh will in the years feed roots of blood-red roses.

Yes, this million of young workmen slaughtered one another and never saw their red hands.

And oh, it would have been a great job of killing and a new and beautiful thing under the sun if the million knew why they hacked and tore each other to death.

The kings are grinning, the kaiser and the czar—they are alive riding in leather-seated motor cars, and they have their women and roses for ease, and they eat fresh poached eggs for breakfast, new butter on toast, sitting in tall water-tight houses reading the news of war.

I dreamed a million ghosts of the young workmen rose in their shirts all soaked in crimson ... and yelled:

God damn the grinning kings, God damn the kaiser and the czar.

Chicago, 1915

🍀 In The Shadow of the Palace

Let us go out of the fog, John, out of the filmy persistent drizzle on
the streets of Stockholm, let us put down the collars of our
raincoats, take off our hats and sit in the newspaper office.

Let us sit among the telegrams—clickety-click—the kaiser's crown
goes into the gutter and the Hohenzollern throne of a thousand
years falls to pieces a one-hoss shay.

It is a fog night out and the umbrellas are up and the collars of the
raincoats—and all the steamboats up and down the Baltic sea
have their lights out and the wheelsmen sober.

Here the telegrams come—one king goes and another—butter is
costly: there is no butter to buy for our bread in Stockholm—
and a little patty of butter costs more than all the crowns of
Germany.

Let us go out in the fog, John, let us roll up our raincoat collars and
go on the streets where men are sneering at the kings.

🍀 The Four Brothers

Notes for War Songs (November, 1917)

Make war songs out of these;
Make chants that repeat and weave.
Make rhythms up to the ragtime chatter of the machine guns;

Make slow-booming psalms up to the boom of the big guns.
Make a marching song of swinging arms and swinging legs,
    Going along,
    Going along,
On the roads from San Antonio to Athens, from Seattle to Bagdad—
The boys and men in winding lines of khaki, the circling squares of
    bayonet points.

Cowpunchers, cornhuskers, shopmen, ready in khaki;
Ballplayers, lumberjacks, ironworkers, ready in khaki;
A million, ten million, singing, "I am ready."
This the sun looks on between two seaboards,
In the land of Lincoln, in the land of Grant and Lee.

I heard one say, "I am ready to be killed."
I heard another say, "I am ready to be killed."
O sunburned clear-eyed boys!
I stand on sidewalks and you go by with drums and guns and bugles,
    You—and the flag!
And my heart tightens, a fist of something feels my throat
    When you go by,
You on the kaiser hunt, you and your faces saying, "I am ready to
    be killed."

They are hunting death,
Death for the one-armed mastoid kaiser.
They are after a Hohenzollern head:
There is no man-hunt of men remembered like this.
The four big brothers are out to kill.
France, Russia, Britain, America—
The four republics are sworn brothers to kill the kaiser.

Yes, this is the great man-hunt;
And the sun has never seen till now
Such a line of toothed and tusked man-killers,

In the blue of the upper sky,
In the green of the undersea,
In the red of winter dawns.
Eating to kill,
Sleeping to kill,
Asked by their mothers to kill,
Wished by four-fifths of the world to kill—
To cut the kaiser's throat,
To hack the kaiser's head,
To hang the kaiser on a high-horizon gibbet.

And is it nothing else than this?
Three times ten million men thirsting the blood
Of a half-cracked one-armed child of the German kings?
Three times ten million men asking the blood
Of a child born with his head wrong-shaped,
The blood of rotted kings in his veins?
If this were all, O God,
I would go to the far timbers
And look on the gray wolves
Tearing the throats of moose:
I would ask a wilder drunk of blood.

Look! It is four brothers in joined hands together.
        The people of bleeding France,
        The people of bleeding Russia,
        The people of Britain, the people of America—
These are the four brothers, these are the four republics.

At first I said it in anger as one who clenches his fist in wrath to fling
    his knuckles into the face of some one taunting;
Now I say it calmly as one who has thought it over and over again
    at night, among the mountains, by the sea-combers in storm.

I say now, by God, only fighters today will save the world, nothing
    but fighters will keep alive the names of those who left red prints
    of bleeding feet at Valley Forge in Christmas snow.
On the cross of Jesus, the sword of Napoleon, the skull of Shake-
    speare, the pen of Tom Jefferson, the ashes of Abraham Lincoln,
    or any sign of the red and running life poured out by the mothers
    of the world,
By the God of morning glories climbing blue the doors of quiet
    homes, by the God of tall hollyhocks laughing glad to children
    in peaceful valleys, by the God of new mothers wishing peace to
    sit at windows nursing babies,
I swear only reckless men, ready to throw away their lives by hun-
    ger, deprivation, desperate clinging to a single purpose imper-
    turbable and undaunted, men with the primitive guts of rebellion,
Only fighters gaunt with the red brand of labor's sorrow on their
    brows and labor's terrible pride in their blood, men with souls
    asking danger—only these will save and keep the four big
    brothers.

Good-night is the word, good-night to the kings, to the czars,
        Good-night to the kaiser.
The breakdown and the fade-away begins.
The shadow of a great broom, ready to sweep out the trash, is here.

One finger is raised that counts the czar,
The ghost who beckoned men who come no more—
The czar gone to the winds on God's great dustpan,
The czar a pinch of nothing,
The last of the gibbering Romanoffs.

Out and good-night—
The ghosts of the summer palaces
And the ghosts of the winter palaces!
Out and out, good-night to the kings, the czars, the kaisers.

Another finger will speak,
And the kaiser, the ghost who gestures a hundred million sleeping-
    waking ghosts,
The kaiser will go onto God's great dustpan—
The last of the gibbering Hohenzollerns.
Look! God pities this trash, God waits with a broom and a dustpan,
God knows a finger will speak and count them out.

It is written in the stars;
It is spoken on the walls;
It clicks in the fire-white zigzag of the Atlantic wireless;
It mutters in the bastions of thousand-mile continents;
It sings in a whistle on the midnight winds from Walla Walla to
    Mesopotamia:
Out and good-night.

The millions slow in khaki,
The millions learning *Turkey in the Straw* and *John Brown's Body*,
The millions remembering windrows of dead at Gettysburg,
    Chickamauga, and Spotsylvania Court House,
The millions dreaming of the morning star of Appomattox,
The millions easy and calm with guns and steel, planes and prows:
        There is a hammering, drumming hell to come.
        The killing gangs are on the way.

God takes one year for a job.
God takes ten years or a million.
God knows when a doom is written.
God knows this job will be done and the words spoken:
Out and good-night.
        The red tubes will run,
        And the great price be paid,
        And the homes empty,
        And the wives wishing,

And the mothers wishing.
There is only one way now, only the way of the red tubes and the
    great price.

    Well . . .
Maybe the morning sun is a five-cent yellow balloon,
And the evening stars the joke of a God gone crazy.
Maybe the mothers of the world,
And the life that pours from their torsal folds—
Maybe it's all a lie sworn by liars,
And a God with a cackling laughter says:
"I, the Almighty God,
I have made all this,
I have made it for kaisers, czars, and kings."

Three times ten million men say: No.
Three times ten million men say:
    God is a God of the People.
And the God who made the world
    And fixed the morning sun,
    And flung the evening stars,
    And shaped the baby hands of life,
This is the God of the Four Brothers;
This is the God of bleeding France and bleeding Russia;
This is the God of the people of Britain and America.

The graves from the Irish Sea to the Caucasus peaks are ten times a
    million.
The stubs and stumps of arms and legs, the eyesockets empty, the
    cripples, ten times a million.
The crimson thumb-print of this anathema is on the door panels of
    a hundred million homes.
Cows gone, mothers on sick-beds, children cry a hunger and no milk
    comes in the noon-time or at night.

The death-yells of it all, the torn throats of men in ditches calling
    for water, the shadows and the hacking lungs in dugouts, the steel
    paws that clutch and squeeze a scarlet drain day by day—the
    storm of it is hell.
But look! child! the storm is blowing for a clean air.

Look! the four brothers march
And hurl their big shoulders
And swear the job shall be done.

Out of the wild finger-writing north and south, east and west, over
    the blood-crossed, blood-dusty ball of earth,
Out of it all a God who knows is sweeping clean,
Out of it all a God who sees and pierces through, is breaking and
    cleaning out an old thousand years, is making ready for a new
    thousand years.
The four brothers shall be five and more.

Under the chimneys of the winter-time the children of the world
    shall sing new songs.
Among the rocking restless cradles the mothers of the world shall
    sing new sleepy-time songs.

❧ *Nearer Than Any Mother's Heart Wishes*

I

In the month of February Eighteen Sixty One
there was a saint in Charleston, South Carolina
and everybody loved him for what he had of
humor, patience, understanding, compassion:
he was soft and hard and nobody's fool,
standing over six feet, heavy jowls, big mouth,

swarthy skin, oily black hair straight
down the slope of his broad back.
   And he sees war coming North and South.
He meets a man one morning asking him which way
to the Lunatic Asylum—and James Louis Petigru
answers by pointing north, south, east, and west:
   "Go any way at all—you can't go wrong—
   The whole country has gone crazy!"

   2

After Ghengis Khan had burned a thousand barns,
wrecked a hundred towns, and killed and killed
more people than he had time to count
he heard an old peasant woman say one day:
"Now this here Ghengis Khan where did he come
   from? I never heard of him."
And it changed his ideas about name and fame.

   3

After Napoleon had crossed one country
and let them know who he was
people looked at what was left
of the homes and crops, saying:
"Next year the roses will be more blood-red.
It was like that after the last war."
And yet Napoleon—what did he know about war?
And does he look like an amateur today?
Did he ever see motorized units whirling
Over hard roads with troop replacements?
Or tanks giving cavalry the horselaugh?
Or a roving skyrider with a load of TNT?
Or an undersea boat releasing a torpedo?

Or a machine gun brigade landing from parachutes?
Or a rolling yellow wall of mustard gas
guaranteed to make them cry and mow them down?
Or civilian populations drilled for air raids?
Napoleon yes he could come back and take lessons.
And Sherman, old William Tecumseh, he too could come
back and say, "War is hell and stinks worse than ever."

4

Think about anything cold now
for the sake of keeping cool.
    Be a piece of ice.
Think about yourself as a long icicle.
Think about the winter northern lights,
shivering splinters of the aurora borealis.
Consider the Arctics: tell yourself a story
about someone just a little coo-coo
climbing the North Pole for the view
        wearing an ice hat
        where the nights are six months long.

5

Advice is cheap: in one ear and out the other.
And you can hear anything you want to hear.
And this is a free country and you can walk
right up to any other man and say:
"Excuse me while I give you an earful."
And furthermore this being a free country
he can tell you when you are through:
"Where have I heard that chatter before?"
This happens every day in a time when
garrulous man never before had so many things

whereby to be garrulous:
billboards by day, neon signs by night,
telegraph, telephone, teletype, ticker tape,
phonograph recordings, electrical transcriptions,
extra extry uxtra newspaper mister the latest,
sound films, sound trucks, newsreels,
amplifiers, public address systems, loud speakers,
skywriting airplanes mentioning dog food,
undersea cables and transoceanic phone and wireless,
high fidelity transmitters of your slightest word,
your cough or your whisper in the little mike
going coast to coast and to other continents.

    And the head of man, the noggin, the bean,
    the reservoir located above the ears,
    the top floor seething, swarming, alive,
    the little garret sometimes half empty
    and only a few crippled bats flying—
into these rooms of the human brain they launch
their loads of propaganda and call it good—
torpedoes of hate germs, plasms of passion—
unimpeachable giant facts glibly twisted into
shuddering fantasies of dripping maniac dwarfs—
honest questions of common men answered with lies—
unanswerable questions given slimy adroit answers—
stuffed prophets strutting their stuff—
minor mouthpieces imitating the majors—
one Manhattan bureau of public relations saying:
"We can make the people believe anything we want
    them to."
Nevertheless one Sunday morning leaving St. Joe, Missouri
a brakeman, a stinger, walks into the smoker
and flops himself alongside a fireman in overalls,

alongside a tallowpot bothering nobody, asking with a grin,
  "What do you know today for sure?"
And the answer came with a grin and a slow finality:
  "Not a damn thing."

The innocent bystander is not always so innocent
as he looks: he can tell a hawk from a handsaw
and is ready to swear on a stack of Bibles that
a horse chestnut and a chestnut horse are never
the same: he may ask "Is that so?" and if you
prove it then ask "What of it?" having notions
of his own: he is careless slinging grammar around
knowing "Some of 'em that ain't sayin' ain't ain't eatin'."

                    6

There are ideas tied up with dreams.
Too often these dreams are wild and crazy.
They get going in the blood of men.
    Then history begins popping.
    Then hell breaks loose.
    Fast or slow the hell spends itself.
Then everybody takes a rest and wonders
when and where hell will break loose next.
This is the chart of the fever and curse
of pre-war, war, post-war, and again later
pre-war, war, post-war.

                    7

Any mother might be hearing her boy child now asking:
"Mama what is this supreme sacrifice I hear about?"
And answering, "Supreme sacrifice is when you go to
    war and die for your country."

Any mother might be saying now:
"The cool music of deep hearts is on me.
The fathoms of ancient fears are on me."

Nearer than any mother's heart wishes
now is heartbreak time.

8

Be steady now and keep your shirt on
like George Washington did when
he heard the crying out loud in his time—
would that be good advice?

Be cool as death now
Like Old Abe Lincoln kept cool
when a hurricane began snarling—
would that be good advice?

Try to figure it out for yourself
remembering figures can lie
and liars can figure
and some promises are not worth
the paper they are written on.

They are changing the maps
of Europe, Asia, and Africa—
they are changing the maps like always.

Over pieces of land they are wrangling,
over iron and oil and fat lands,
over breed and kin and race pride,
over poisons, balloons, baboon reachings—
 and the little wars are leading on
 into the big war to come.

Who could have given us the lowdown
on why Mussolini
poured troops and planes into Spain?

Who explained why Hitler
threw heavy guns and flying bombers
to the help of Franco
and the Mohammedan Moors of France
and the cause of Liberty and God in Spain
and the iron works
and the mineral deposits of Spain?
      How will his slogans die
      and his abracadabra vanish?

    9

Be steady now and keep your shirt on.
    Be cool as death if you can.
Try to figure it out for yourself.

    Behind this awful music
is a more awful music to come?
They are changing the maps like always.

    Study the make of a gas mask
    how to wear it over your face
    how to conduct yourself wearing it
in rooms and streets, in your daily doings.

    They gaze as silent baboons
    in the guise of long snouts
though under this outer guise they are
human wanderers with nostrils seeking
    air, oxygen, freedom, peace.

Under the fantasies of these skulls
runs the hope of human dignity
                        somehow, sometime.

            10

    Presents are delivered from the sky,
        in every package a prize, a chance,
        to choke, to suffocate, to forget
    yes to forget every last word ever spoken of
    man higher in the scale than animal creation,
    the gorilla and the tiger being mere beasts
    while man has shrines, altars, lights,
    books awarding him personal immortality,
        books not yet banned nor burned.

    Let yourself be
    imperturbable as brass candlesticks
    or ancient folios bound in leather
    holding common prayers on parchment
        with the calm of an ivory crucifix when
    shattered glass showers the chairs, the floor, the desk,
    splinters and dust of glass cover the bath-tub bottom,
    when plaster drops on the breakfast cloth
    not long before the walls hesitate and totter
    and the roof caves in (as in Hangkow or Canton),
    when (as in Madrid) the sirens sound and the ambulances
    pick up in the streets the mutilated still breathing
    and carry them to hospitals not yet bombed and wrecked.

        Few of us will take it
        and say it is good
        The old wars were
        something else again.

Now babies will have baby-size gas masks.

> The time to be hard and bitter
> —is that time now?
> Or shall we insist on asking now the
> ancient question:
> "What do the people get for the wars
> they fight with each other?"

11

> The human heart weaves consolations.
> And they are made of what?
> Of thin air—of the blue substance of the
> shadows of bones—
> of a stuff so finespun it has the heft of mist,
> merely mist
> or the desperate balance between discipline and
> freedom.

> Men fight for dreams of freedom
> finding later they fought for
> land, for trade routes, for empire,
> for markets and controls,
> for gains in cash and dominance.

Yet again men fight for dreams of freedom
and win footholds for human rights,
measurable gains for mankind:
in the strife of strikes and wars
> > sometimes this happens
> > as a poem of action
> > long remembered.

1 2

Now in the looking glass of our time
now we have seen rehearsals for what?

   The grinning cats of accomplished fact
   sit wiping their faces.
Thus it was in Shanghai, in Bilbao, in Ethiopia,
   in Vienna on the blue Danube.

   The story keeps going:
   a serial to be concluded
sometime in the rolling of the ivories,
   in the shuffling of cards,
in the heads-or-tails of circumstance,
   sometime.

   Some had names and numbers.
   They are rubbed out.
To them came the bloody trucks
   and the published orders
   and the secret arrests
   and the public atrocities
   and the studied punishments
   of concentration camps.

   Day by day they march—
   the living dead men
   remembering dimly how
   they had freedom:
"and the next day it rained."

1 3

   The crying of red flowers
   is to come in the sky.

Farther yet the revolving blossoms
  of the bombing squadrons.

  Spain shall spread.
  China shall not be alone.
  Neither Addis Ababa nor liberty
  is a final and willing corpse.

  Too many corpses refused to be
  final and willing corpses.
They talk now in their last sleep:
  and they are heard:
  these losers are heard.

  The earth may yet seem covered with losers.
Nevertheless before the last platoon of losers is shot,
Before the last corpse gets a storm-trooper kick in the face
There will be fresh foreshadowings on the air.
  For the winners never win in this game
  and keep their winnings: it is so written.
  Corpses can be flung in a hole:
                    shadows march on.

  The losers so often come back
  ghosting their conquerors.
  There are not nails enough
  to nail down victory.
No more can absolute conquest be kept without change
than you can take wool and weave garments for shadows.

  Spain yes, China yes, Austria ja:
  they are beginnings:
  yet to come is the drama and its Act I,
    Act II, Act III—and so on.

Their lost men took a hand so often
in items of sheer valor, no music nor flowers,
dying without witnesses nor loved ones at hand
    nor enough fragments
    to put in a basket for burial.

You young ones, you darlings of destiny,
before your eyes too
shall unfold the sheets of fire and the call:
        popular fronts and governments
        shall not perish from the earth:
        is this the word? this from
        that shovel of dust and valor in Spain—
even though a fraction of them had only a notion
to take a whirl at the wild game of war
and flirt with death for the fun of it?

The timing of their laughter
may be mentioned—
those who spat in the dust
saying, "What the hell? Who wants
        to live forever anyhow?"

    1 4

    One may speak as no prophet at all,
        as a traveler taking it slow
        over a mug of java with ham on rye,
as a citizen troubled over storm warnings,
over black roses, heavy roses in the sky,
and heavy heavy heavy hangs over thy head.

        They are changing the maps
        of Europe, Asia, Africa,
they are changing the maps like always.

Be steady now and keep your shirt on.
        Be cool as death if you can.
Try to figure it out for yourself.

The lilacs of April are good to look at.
So are the oaks of gold in the fall of the year
And the whirl of snow in the winter time
        and the growing corn in summer.
They carry beautiful fables
        for those having time to look and see.

And yet—what of it? who cares?
When young men are cut down like cornstalks
and cathedrals go down like oaks under lightning
and lilacs wither from the breath of gas—
        what of it? who cares?

        When shall men be hard and bitter,
        open and public and incessant
        in the asking of that terrible question:
"What do the people get for the wars they fight
        with each other?"

Any mother might be saying now:
"The cool music of deep hearts is on me.
The fathoms of ancient fears are on me."

Nearer than any mother's heart wishes
now is heartbreak time.

        1938

Open Letter to the Poet Archibald MacLeish Who Has Forsaken His Massachusetts Farm to Make Propaganda for Freedom

Thomas Jefferson had red hair and a violin
and he loved life and people and music
and books and writing and quiet thoughts—
a lover of peace, decency, good order,
summer corn ripening for the bins of winter,
cows in green pastures, colts sucking at mares,
apple trees waiting to laugh with pippins—
Jefferson loved peace like a good farmer.
And yet—for eight years he fought in a war—
writing with his own hand the war announcement
named The Declaration of Independence
making The Fourth of July a sacred calendar date.
And there was his friend and comrade
Ben Franklin, the printer, bookman, diplomat:
all Franklin asked was they let him alone
so he could do his work as lover of peace and work—
Franklin too made war for eight years—
the same Franklin who said two nations
would better throw dice than go to war—
he threw in with fighters for freedom—
for eight years he threw in all he had:
the books, the printshop, fun with electricity,

searches and researches in science pure and applied—
these had to wait while he joined himself
to eight long years of war for freedom, independence.

> Now, of course, these two odd fellows
> stand as only two among many:
> the list runs long of these fellows,
> lovers of peace, decency, good order,
> who throw in with all they've got
> for the abstractions "freedom," "independence."
> Strictly they were gentle men, not hunting trouble.
> Strictly they wanted quiet, the good life, freedom.
> They would rather have had the horses of instruction
> those eight years they gave to the tigers of wrath.
> The record runs they were both dreamers
> at the same time they refused imitations of the real thing
> at the same time they stood up and talked back
> at the same time they met the speech of steel and cunning with
> their own relentless steel and cunning.

1940

❧ *The Man with the Broken Fingers*

(When this tale of methodically inflicted agony was published in The Chicago
Times Syndicate newspapers August 23, 1942, it brought inquiries whether it was
war propaganda or based on an actual incident. My informant was a Norwegian
ski champion known as Lieutenant "Andreas" for the safety of his home kinfolk.
He gave the incident as he had it from the son of the main tragic figure. Among
many other related points was one of German soldiers whose minds began to
crack under the strain of the inhuman acts required of them by their superiors,
such soldiers being returned to Germany as "mental cases" needing therapeutic
treatment. "Andreas," a sober and modest hero, was killed in a bomber flight

over Berlin. Friends of "Andreas" say the story below had translation into other languages and circulation by undergrounds.)

The Man with the Broken Fingers throws a shadow.
Down from the spruce and evergreen mountain timbers of
    Norway—
And across Europe and the Mediterranean to the oasis palms of
    Libya—
He lives and speaks a sign language of lost fingers.
From a son of Norway who slipped the Gestapo nets, the Nazi
    patrols,
The story comes as told among those now in Norway.

Shrines in their hearts they have for this nameless man
Who refused to remember names names names the Gestapo
    wanted.
"Tell us these names. Who are they? Talk! We want those names!"
And the man faced them, looked them in the eye, and hours passed
    and no names came—hours on hours and no names for the
    Gestapo.
They told him they would break him as they had broken others.
The rubber hose slammed around face and neck,
The truncheon handing pain with no telltale marks,
Or the distinction of the firing squad and death in a split second—
The Gestapo considered these and decided for him something else
    again.
"Tell us those names. Who were they? Talk! Names now—or
    else!"
And no names came—over and over and no names.

So they broke the little finger of the left hand.
Three fingers came next and the left thumb bent till it broke.
Still no names and there was a day and night for rest and thinking
    it over.

Then again the demand for names and he gave them the same
    silence.
And the little finger of the right hand felt itself twisted,
Back and back twisted till it hung loose from a bleeding socket.
Then three more fingers crashed and splintered one by one
And the right thumb back and back into shattered bone.

Did he think about violins or accordions he would never touch
    again?
Did he think of baby or woman hair he would never again play
    with?
Or of hammers or pencils no good to him any more?
Or of gloves and mittens that would always be misfits?
He may have laughed half a moment over a Gestapo job
So now for a while he would handle neither knife nor fork
Nor lift to his lips any drinking-cup handle
Nor sign his name with a pen between thumb and fingers.

And all this was halfway—there was more to come.
The Gestapo wit and craft had an aim.
They wanted it known in Norway the Gestapo can be terrible.
They wanted a wide whispering of fear
Of how the Nazis handle those who won't talk or tell names.
"We give you one more chance to co-operate."
Yet he had no names for them.
His locked tongue, his Norwegian will pitted against Nazi will,
His pride and faith in a free man's way,
His welcoming death rather than do what they wanted—
They brought against this their last act of fury,
Breaking the left arm at the elbow,
Breaking it again at the shoulder socket—
And when he came to in a flicker of opening eyes
They broke the right arm first at the elbow, then the shoulder.
By now of course he had lost all memory of names, even his own.

And there are those like you and me and many many others
Who can never forget the Man with the Broken Fingers.
His will, his pride as a free man, shall go on.
His shadow moves and his sacred fingers speak.
He tells men there are a thousand writhing shattering deaths
Better to die one by one than to say yes yes yes
When the answer is no no no and death is welcome and death
    comes soon
And death is a quiet step into a sweet clean midnight.

August 23, 1942

🌱 Forgotten Wars

Be loose. Be easy. Be ready.
Forget the last war.
Forget the one before.
Forget the one yet to come.

Be loose and easy about the wars
whether they have been fought
or whether yet to be fought—
be ready to forget them.

Who was saying at high noon today:
"Is not each of them a forgotten war
after it is fought and over?
how and why it came forgotten?
how and what it cost forgotten?
and was he there at Iwo Jima, Okinawa
or places named Cassino, Anzio, the Bulge?
and saying now:

"Let the next war before it comes
and before it gets under way
and five or six days sees its finish
or fifty years sees it still going strong
—let it be now a forgotten war.
    Be ready now to forget it.
    Be loose, be easy now.
The next war goes over in a flash—or runs long."

 Grass

Pile the bodies high at Austerlitz and Waterloo.
Shovel them under and let me work—
              I am the grass; I cover all.

And pile them high at Gettysburg
And pile them high at Ypres and Verdun.
Shovel them under and let me work.
Two years, ten years, and passengers ask the conductor:
             What place is this?
             Where are we now?

             I am the grass.
             Let me work.

PORTRAITS

. . . *Reedy had encouraged Masters to read* Epigrams from the Greek
Anthology. *Masters and Sandburg spoke of the book that spring [of
1914] on their walks and talks, and read and reread it. It prompted
Sandburg to write "many early portrait poems," according to Paula
[Sandburg's wife].*

— PENELOPE NIVEN, from *Carl Sandburg:
A Biography*

🌺 To a Poet*

You said I would go alone,
I would find my way.
But you were the strongest person I had known.
You were the morning wind, and you were stone.
You said: I know that you will go your way.
Whatever horse you want to ride is yours,
And night is yours, and the evening gleams, and day.
I can tell you nothing you have not known.
I said: I go with you; I am your own.
But I went alone.

🌺 Memoir of a Proud Boy

He lived on the wings of storm.
The ashes are in Chihuahua.

Out of Ludlow and coal towns in Colorado
Sprang a vengeance of Slav miners, Italians, Scots, Cornishmen,
    Yanks
Killings ran under the spoken commands of this boy
With eighty men and rifles on a hogback mountain.

*Sandburg attended Lombard College from 1898–1902, and was deeply influenced by
Professor Philip Green Wright, the poet referred to in the title.

They killed swearing to remember
The shot and charred wives and children
In the burnt camp of Ludlow,
And Louis Tikas, the laughing Greek,
Plugged with a bullet, clubbed with a gun butt.

As a home war
It held the nation a week
And one or two million men stood together
And swore by the retribution of steel.

It was all accidental.
He lived flecking lint off coat lapels
Of men he talked with.
He kissed the miners' babies
And wrote a Denver paper
Of picket silhouettes on a mountain line.

He had no mother but Mother Jones
Crying from a jail window of Trinidad:
"All I want is room enough to stand
And shake my fist at the enemies of the human race."

Named by a grand jury as a murderer
He went to Chihuahua, forgot his old Scotch name,
Smoked cheroots with Pancho Villa
And wrote letters of Villa as a rock of the people.

How can I tell how Don MacGregor went?

Three riders emptied lead into him.
He lay on the main street of an inland town.
A boy sat near all day throwing stones
To keep pigs away.

The Villa men buried him in a pit
With twenty Carranzistas.

There is drama in that point . . .
. . . the boy and the pigs.
Griffith would make a movie of it to fetch sobs.
Victor Herbert would have the drums whirr
In a weave with a high fiddle-string's single clamor.

"And the muchacho sat there all day throwing stones
To keep the pigs away," wrote Gibbons to the *Tribune*.

Somewhere in Chihuahua or Colorado
Is a leather bag of poems and short stories.

❧ *Napoleon*

The little boy blew bubbles
Floating the air to glisten and shine
With a rainbow joy and airiness silken:
   They floated and broke and were gone.

The man blew bubbles,
Made nations and kings and captains
And armies that marched and slaughtered
And laughed at the blood on their hands—
   But the armies and kings and captains
   Are broken and vanished and gone.

❧ *Hawthorne*

Nathaniel Hawthorne lived under an arch of glooms.
Invisible scarves of undertaker's crepe
Twisted at his throat to fasten on him
And he fought forever lifelong
The winds whipping to fasten these scarves.

Between two ears under a bone dome: caverns,
Or if we so choose: dank tarns:
And here he swam forever lifelong
Round and round in the destiny of a brass bowl
Lined with an inner dark of sea-green tarnish.

The wind whipping those scarves, of course,
Is another metaphor.

❧ *Mr. Blake's Chariots*

Mr. Blake saw invisible chariots on the sky
driven by unseen charioteers.
Himself he saw as a slim wisp of an ashen
mortality
And nevertheless took himself for a charioteer
riding high, grand and lonely.

Evidence As to a She Devil

Socrates had a fool woman.
She ragged him, nagged him.
Her initial was X for Xantippe.
Socrates learned about women from her.
She was a shrew, a virago, a hell cat.
       So they say.
       So-they-say.
What we know is what they say.
We do not know what Xantippe would reply
If asked, why did you rag and nag Socrates?
She might say he was lousy and bring evidence.
She might lie till we saw she was a regular liar.
She might show him as lazy, gabby, no provider.
Or she might hurl many furious useless words
Till she sounded like a leather-tongued scold.
We know only what they say.
       We have not heard from Xantippe herself.

🌿 Arms

(For Wallace Stevens)

Renoir goes on painting.
A man from south France tells me it is so.
One picture a day, good or bad, the old man goes on.
And a little work every day on one big picture for God
    and children and remembered women.
So Renoir, his right arm no good anymore
And the left arm half gone,
So Renoir goes on.

And when you come again
We will go to the Edelweiss for jazz
Or to Hester's dirty place on the river
Or to some Chinese dump where they bring what you want
    and no questions asked,
And I will ask you why Renoir does it
And I believe you will tell me.

🌿 Eugene V. Debs

On his face as he lay, at peace at last, in Terre Haute,
There was the majestic trajectory of a trail from the earth
to the stars.

The cotillions of the Milky Way could not bewilder him
by their numbers.
He had always dreamed of paths difficult for human feet,
bridges impossible to the calculations of accepted
engineers, union depots open to all the races and languages
of man.
He was a railroad man, familiar to the link and coupling
pin, to rain, zero weather, snow plows, stalled engines, the
first Brotherhood of Railroad Firemen, the first American
Railway Union.
He was an orator, a jailbird, a presidential candidate, an
enemy of war, a convict, a philosopher, storyteller, friend
of man.
Said a poet, "He had ten hopes to your one."

A sister laid a spray of four Crusader red roses
on his breast.

Over in Valhalla, if Valhalla is not demolished, rebuilt,
renamed, he speaks at ease with Garrison, John Brown,
Albert Parsons, Spartacus.

🍀 *Ezra**

Good reading good reading
O most excellent reading
If can easy pass over
Easy skip idiotics
    pedantics pomposities
Good reading sure sure

*The poet Ezra Pound.

I have learnt
　　how to read Ez
He is my crazy brudder

🐛 *Good Babies Make Good Poems*

Doctor Williams having delivered
eleven hundred babies
in Rutherford New Jersey
also delivered from himself
eleven hundred poems
each poem a baby
to grow up and please the Doctor
and give him pride in himself
as the mother of each baby
and himself her obstetrician
thus having two prides
ever pleasing his heart—
one the embryo poem
in his fertile brain-womb—
the other his obstetric skill
with no use of forceps
delivering the brain-child
to wriggle in black ink on white paper
Doctor Williams saying often to himself,
　　　"Good babies make good poems."

❧ From an Illinois Prairie Hut

For Amy Lowell

She regrets a lost town in Vermont,
lost streets of her childhood town in Vermont;
grassroots tugging at the streets and taking Main Street
of her childhood town, the old home town, in Vermont,
    these she regrets,
      and each regret is a grassroot
      and a grassroot must be strong and bitter.

She regrets a horse chestnut,
a tree with a torso ten people join hands and circle round,
a buckeye dying, a tough and beautiful horse chestnut dying,
she regrets this storm of white blossoms will not paint the summer
   sky when the buckeye is gone—
      and each regret
      is a high thin goose of autumn
      crying south, crying south.

She fixes the millimeters of her glasses herself;
She measures the curve of her eyesight wishing to measure
The curve of the arch of the sky of night, the curve of the
   running hours on the level of night,
And the moon stumbles of early morning and the testimony of
   the dawn across the first light sheets.
She measures the millimeters of her eyesight with regrets
      and each regret is a grassroot

and each regret is a high thin goose of autumn crying
south.

🌺 Letters to Dead Imagists

Emily Dickinson:
You gave us the bumblebee who has a soul,
The everlasting traveler among the hollyhocks,
And how God plays around a back yard garden.

Stevie Crane:
War is kind and we never knew the kindness of war till you came;
Nor the black riders and clashes of spear and shield out of the sea,
Nor the mumblings and shots that rise from dreams on call.

🌺 Illinois Farmer

Bury this old Illinois farmer with respect.
He slept the Illinois nights of his life after days of work in Illinois
    cornfields.
Now he goes on a long sleep.
The wind he listened to in the cornsilk and the tassels, the wind that
    combed his red beard zero mornings when the snow lay white on
    the yellow ears in the bushel basket at the corncrib,
The same wind will now blow over the place here where his hands
    must dream of Illinois corn.

🐟 *Osawatomie*

I don't know how he came,
shambling, dark, and strong.

He stood in the city and told men:
My people are fools, my people are young and strong, my people
      must learn, my people are terrible workers and fighters.
Always he kept on asking: Where did that blood come from?

    They said: You for the fool killer,
         you for the booby hatch
         and a necktie party.

    They hauled him into jail.
    They sneered at him and spit on him,
    And he wrecked their jails,
    Singing, "God damn your jails,"
    And when he was most in jail
    Crummy among the crazy in the dark
    Then he was most of all out of jail
    Shambling, dark, and strong,
Always asking: Where did that blood come from?
    They laid hands on him
    And the fool killers had a laugh
    And the necktie party was a go, by God.
They laid hands on him and he was a goner.
    They hammered him to pieces and he stood up.
They buried him and he walked out of the grave, by God,
    Asking again: Where did that blood come from?

🍀 *Grieg Being Dead*

Grieg being dead we may speak of him and his art.
Grieg being dead we can talk about whether he was any good
    or not.
Grieg being with Ibsen, Björnson, Lief Ericson and the rest,
Grieg being dead does not care a hell's hoot what we say.

      Morning, Spring, Anitra's Dance,
      He dreams them at the doors of new stars.

🍀 *Sherwood Anderson*

To write one book in five years
or five books in one year,
to be the painter and the thing painted,
the writer and the written of
—where are we, bo?

Wait. Get the number of this guy.

The barbershop handling is not all
nor the tweeds, the cheviot, the Scotch mist,
nor the flame orange scarf.

On looks he is "bushwah"*—

*bourgeois.

And yet—he sleeps under bridges with lonely
crazy men; he sits in country jails with icono-
clasts and sab cats*; he drinks beer with broken-
down burlesque actresses; he has cried with a
heart full of tears for Windy MacPherson's father;
he draws pencil sketches of the wrists of lonely
women whose flowers are ashes.

Can a man sit at a desk in a skyscraper in Chicago, Illinois,
and be a harnessmaker in a corn town in Iowa
and feel the tall grass coming up in June
and the ache of the cottonwood trees
singing with the prairie wind?

Ask this guy. Get his number.

Jack London and O. Henry

Both were jailbirds; no speechmakers at all;
speaking best with one foot on a brass rail;
a beer glass in the left hand and the right
hand employed for gestures.

And both were lights snuffed out . . . no warning
. . . no lingering:
Who knew the hearts of these boozefighters?

*sab cat—a logger's name for an expert at sabotage; named for the black cat pictured on
an I.W.W. emblem.

❧ *Without the Cane and the Derby*

(For C. C.)*

The woman had done him wrong.

Either that . . . or the woman was clean as a white rose in the morning gauze of dew.

It was either one or the other or it was the two things, right and wrong, woven together like two braids of a woman's head of hair hanging down woven together.

The room is dark. The door opens. It is Charlie playing for his friends after dinner, "the marvelous urchin, the little genius of the screen," (chatter it like a monkey's running laughter cry.)

No . . . it is not Charlie . . . it is somebody else. It is a man, gray shirt, bandana, dark face. A candle in his left hand throws a slant of light on the dark face. The door closes slow. The right hand leaves the door knob slow.

He looks at something. What is it? A white sheet on a table. He takes two long soft steps. He runs the candle light around a hump in the sheet. He lifts the sheet slow, sad like.

A woman's head of hair shows, a woman's white face. He takes the head between his hands and looks long at it. His fingers trickle under the sheet, snap loose something, bring out fingers full of a pearl necklace.

He covers the face and the head of hair with the white sheet. He takes a step toward the door. The necklace slips into his pocket

*Charlie Chaplin.

off the fingers of his right hand. His left hand lifts the candle for a good-by look.

Knock, knock, knock. A knocking the same as the time of the human heartbeat.

Knock, knock, knock, first louder, then lower. Knock, knock, knock, the same as the time of the human heartbeat.

He sets the candle on the floor . . . leaps to the white sheet . . . rips it back . . . has his fingers at the neck, his thumbs at the throat, and does three slow fierce motions of strangling.

The knocking stops. All is quiet. He covers the face and the head of hair with the white sheet, steps back, picks up the candle and listens.

Knock, knock, knock, a knocking the same as the time of the human heartbeat.

Knock, knock, knock, first louder, then lower. Knock, knock, knock, the same as the time of the human heartbeat.

Again the candle to the floor, the leap, the slow fierce motions of strangling, the cover-up of the face and the head of hair, the step back, the listening.

And again the knock, knock, knock . . . louder . . . lower . . . to the time of the human heartbeat.

Once more the motions of strangling . . . then . . . nothing at all . . . nothing at all . . . no more knocking . . . no knocking at all . . . no knocking at all . . . in the time of the human heartbeat.

He stands at the door . . . peace, peace, peace everywhere only in the man's face so dark and his eyes so lighted up with many lights, no peace at all, no peace at all.

So he stands at the door, his right hand on the door knob, the candle slants of light fall and flicker from his face to the straight white sheet changing gray against shadows.

So there is peace everywhere . . . no more knocking . . . no knocking
at all to the time of the human heartbeat . . . so he stands at the
door and his right hand on the door knob.
And there is peace everywhere . . . only the man's face is a red gray
plaster of storm in the center of peace . . . so he stands with a
candle at the door . . . so he stands with a red gray face.

After he steps out the door closes; the door, the door knob, the table,
the white sheet, there is nothing at all; the owners are shadows;
the owners are gone; not even a knocking; not even a knock,
knock, knock . . . louder, lower, in the time of the human
heartbeat.
The lights are snapped on. Charlie, "the marvelous urchin, the little
genius of the screen" (chatter it with a running monkey's laugh-
ter cry) Charlie is laughing a laugh the whole world knows.
The room is full of cream yellow lights. Charlie is laughing . . .
louder . . . lower . . .
And again the heartbeats laugh . . . the human heartbeats laugh. . . .

❧ *To the Ghost of John Milton*

If I should pamphleteer twenty years against royalists,
With rewards offered for my capture dead or alive,
And jails and scaffolds always near,

And then my wife should die and three ignorant daughters
Should talk about their father as a joke, and steal the
Earnings of books, and the poorhouse always reaching for
          me,

If I then lost my eyes and the world was all dark and I
Sat with only memories and talk—

I would write "Paradise Lost," I would marry a second wife
And on her dying I would marry a third pair of eyes to
Serve my blind eyes, I would write "Paradise Regained," I
Would write wild, foggy, smoky, wordy books—

I would sit by the fire and dream of hell and heaven,
Idiots and kings, women my eyes could never look on again,
And God Himself and the rebels God threw into hell.

Mysterious Biography

Christofo Colombo was a hungry man,
hunted himself half way round the world;
he began poor, panhandled, ended in jail,
Christofo so hungry, Christofo so poor,
Christofo in the chilly, steel bracelets,
honorable distinguished Christofo Colombo.

Mr. Longfellow and His Boy

(An old-fashioned recitation to be read aloud)

Mr. Longfellow, Henry Wadsworth Longfellow,
    the Harvard Professor,
    the poet whose pieces you see in all the schoolbooks,
"Tell me not in mournful numbers
    life is but an empty dream . . ."
Mr. Longfellow sits in his Boston library writing,

Mr. Longfellow looks across the room
        and sees his nineteen-year-old boy
propped up in a chair at a window,
home from the war,
a rifle ball through right and left shoulders.

In his diary the father writes about his boy:
        "He has a wound through him a foot long.
        He pretends it does not hurt him."
And the father if he had known
would have told the boy propped up in a chair
how one of the poems written in that room
        made President Lincoln cry.
And both the father and the boy
would have smiled to each other and felt good
about why the President had tears over that poem.

Noah Brooks, the California newspaperman,
could have told the Longfellows how one day
Brooks heard the President saying two lines:
        "Thou, too, sail on, O Ship of State!
        Sail on, O Union, strong and great!"
Noah Brooks, remembering more of the poem, speaks:
        "Thou, too, sail on, O Ship of State!
        Sail on, O Union, strong and great!
        Humanity with all its fears,
        With all the hopes of future years,
        Is hanging breathless on thy fate!
        We know what Master laid thy keel,
        What workmen wrought thy ribs of steel,
        Who made each mast, and sail, and rope,
        What anvils rang, what hammers beat,
        In what a forge and what a heat

Were shaped the anchors of thy hope!
Fear not each sudden sound and shock,
'Tis of the wave and not the rock;
'Tis but the flapping of the sail,
And not a rent made by the gale!
In spite of rock and tempest's roar,
In spite of false lights on the shore,
Sail on, nor fear to breast the sea!
Our hearts, our hopes, are all with thee,
Our hearts, our hopes, our prayers, our tears,
Our faith triumphant o'er our fears,
Are all with thee—are all with thee!"

Noah Brooks sees Lincoln's eyes filled with tears,
        the cheeks wet.
They sit quiet a little while, then Lincoln saying:
"It is a wonderful gift to be able to stir men like that."
Mr. Longfellow—and his boy sitting propped up in a chair—
with a bullet wound a foot long in his shoulders—
would have liked to hear President Lincoln saying
        those words.

Now Mr. Longfellow is gone far away, his boy, too,
        gone far away,
and they never dreamed how seventy-eight years later
the living President of the United States, in the White House at
        Washington,
takes a pen, writes with his own hand on a sheet of paper
about the Union Ship of State sailing on and on—
        never going down—
how the President hands that sheet of paper
to a citizen soon riding high in the air, high over salt water,
high in the rain and the sun and the mist over
        the Atlantic Ocean,

riding, pounding, flying, everything under control,
crossing the deep, wide Atlantic in a day and a night,
coming to London on the Thames in England,
standing before the First Minister of the United Kingdom
so the whole English-language world
from England across North America to Australia and
    New Zealand
can never forget Mr. Longfellow's lines:
    "Thou, too, sail on, O Ship of State!
    Sail on, O Union, strong and great!"

Collier's, June 14, 1941

❧ Dan

Early May, after cold rain the sun baffling cold wind.
Irish setter pup finds a corner near the cellar door,
        all sun and no wind,
Cuddling there he crosses forepaws and lays his skull
Sideways on this pillow, dozing in a half-sleep,
Browns of hazel nut, mahogany, rosewood, played off
        against each other on his paws
        and head.

❧ AFRICAN-AMERICANS

Sandburg is a whole man and his concern with the Negroes' drive for equality and justice has affected every part of him, politically and artistically . . . The problem of racial equality has never been far from Sandburg's mind.

—HARRY GOLDEN, from *Carl Sandburg*

🌿 Jazz Fantasia

Drum on your drums, batter on your banjoes,
sob on the long cool winding saxophones.
Go to it, O jazzmen.

Sling your knuckles on the bottoms of the happy
tin pans, let your trombones ooze, and go husha-
husha-hush with the slippery sand-paper.

Moan like an autumn wind high in the lonesome treetops, moan soft
like you wanted somebody terrible, cry like a racing car slipping
away from a motorcycle cop, bang-bang! you jazzmen, bang alto-
gether drums, traps, banjoes, horns, tin cans—make two people fight
on the top of a stairway and scratch each other's eyes in a clinch
tumbling down the stairs.

Can the rough stuff . . . now a Mississippi steamboat pushes up the
night river with a hoo-hoo-hoo-oo . . . and the green lanterns calling
to the high soft stars . . . a red moon rides on the humps of the low
river hills . . . go to it, O jazzmen.

🌿 Sojourner Truth Speaking

I felt as if I had three hearts
and they were so large
my body could hardly hold them.
    . . .

If my cup won't hold but a pint
and yourn holds a quart,
wouldn't you be mean not to let me have
my little half-measure full?

· · ·

Here you are talking about being
"changed in the twinkling of an eye."
If the Lord should come
He'd change you to *nothing*
for there's nothing to you.

· · ·

Dat little man he say woman
can't have as much rights as man
'cause Christ wasn't a woman.
Whar did your Christ come from? Whar?
From God and a woman.
Man had nothing to do with Him.

· · ·

Jesus will walk with me through the fire
and keep me from harm.
Nothing belonging to God can burn,
any more than God himself.
I shall remain.
Do you tell me
that God's children
can't stand fire?

❧ The People, Yes

55

On Lang Syne Plantation they had a prayer:
"When we rise in the morning
to see the sun plowing his furrow across the elements,
we are thankful.
For the rising of the east moon we have seen tonight
and for the setting of the west moon we shall see,
we are thankful.
And O Lord—
When my room is like a public hall,
when my face is like a looking-glass,
when my teeth shut against a silence,
mother do me no good then,
father do me no good then,
sister, brother, friend, do me no good then.
Help us to know—
when our hands rest from the plow handle and lie still—
when we are like hills gone down in darkness—
when our nostrils are empty of breath—
then let us know when we trust in Thee—

       Thou art a crutch to the lame,
       a mother to the motherless,
       a father to the fatherless,
       a strong arm to the widow,

a shade from the heat,
a bridge over deep water."

[. . .]

Cleo

Born of a slave mother and father, she toiled
in the fields, loved the earth and the sun,
and was strong.

At evening the going down of the sun told her
whether she was written in the book of God as
a good or a bad woman for that day.

In the gloaming of a long autumn day she told
friends, "Every one of us got a baby inside de
body. When de rest of de body shuffle off, dis
baby go to Jesus. Dare is wings waitin' to be
hitched on. Atter dat, you is angel."

The fields and the earth were kind to her.

Black Prophetess

I makes my livin' washin'.
I keeps happy at the feet of Jesus.
My husband ain't saved; he's wicked:
but the Bible says a sanctified wife
shall sanctify her husband and save him.

I'm livin' in Chicago
but I calls Ohio my home
because I lived in Cincinnati
an' Columbus an' Toledo
an' I was in Dayton
a week before the waters swept Dayton
an' I stood on the public square
an' warned 'em of destruction.

I got four permits from the police in Chicago
to stand on the street corners
and warn the people of destruction.
I told 'em about the *Eastland* and the war
before those things happened.

Three years ago the police gave me my last permit
to warn the people of destruction
an' I got a right to stand on any corner
south of Twelfth Street.

They tell me it's a free country
an' I can talk God's destruction all I want
just so I don't come downtown.

I got five daughters.
The oldest is in Philadelphia.
She makes prophecies too.

I make prophecies when the spirit moves me.
Yesterday I felt the spirit stirrin' me up.
I saw blood up to the bridles of the horses.
I saw the mark of the Beast.
(When the Bible speaks of a Beast it means a King.)
The Kings all got to go.

God is cleansing the earth.
He's goin' to make it all clean
and Jesus is goin' to come again
an' live a thousand years.

I go to the newspapers with my prophecies
but they don't print 'em.

If you print this—
when will it be in the paper?

❧ Elizabeth Umpstead

I am Elizabeth Umpstead, dead at seventy-five years of age, and
they are taking me in a polished and silver-plated box today, and an
undertaker, assured of cash for his work, will supply straps to let the
box down the lean dirt walls, while a quartet of singers—assured of
cash for their work, sing "Nearer My God to Thee," and a clergy-
man, also assured of cash for his services—will pronounce the
words: "Dust to dust and ashes to ashes."

I am gone from among the two-legged moving figures on top the
earth now, and nobody will say my heart is someway wrong when I
assert, I was the most beautiful nigger girl in northern Indiana; and
men wanted my beauty, white men and black men—they wanted to
take it and crush it and taste it—and I learned what they wanted
and I traded on it; I schemed and haggled to get all I could for it—
and so, I am one nigger girl who today has a grand funeral with all
the servitors paid in spot cash.

I learned early, away back in short dresses, when a lawyer took
me and used me the same as a brass cuspidor or a new horse and
buggy or a swivel chair or anything that gives more life-ease for
spot cash—he paid $600 cash to me for the keep of the child of my

womb and his loins. And then he went to a revival, sang "Jesus Knows All about Our Troubles," moaned he was a sinner and wanted Jesus to wash his sins away. He joined the church and stood up one night before hundreds of people and blabbed to them how he used me, had a child by me, and paid me $600 cash. And I waited till one night I saw him in the public square and I slashed his face with a leather horsewhip, calling all the wild crazy names that came to my tongue to damn him and damn him and damn him, for a sneak in the face of God and man.

❧ *Sayings of Henry Stephens*

(Springfield, Illinois, 1917)

If you get enough money
you can buy anything
except . . . you got to die.

I don't like meatheads
shootin' off their mouths
always wrasslin' 'n wranglin'.

The cost of things to live on
has gone too high.
They ought to be brung down
where they's more equal like
with other things.

One summer
potatoes was peddled
around Springfield here
for fifty cents a bushel;

another summer
I paid four dollars a bushel.
Tell me why this is.
We got to work to eat.
And the scripture says:
"Muzzle not the ox that
treadeth out the corn."

Human is human.
Human may be wrong
but it's human all the same.
There's time when a scab
ought to have his head knocked off
his shoulders.
But first we ought to talk to him
like a brother.
I pay a dollar a month to the coal miners' union
to help the street car strikers.
It costs me $25 if they ketch me ridin' on a car.
That's all right.
Las' Monday night I busted somethin' in my left arm.
I walked, mind you, I walked a mile and a half
down to the doctor's office.
It kep' on swellin' an' when I got home
my wife had to put salt and vinegar on
to get my sleeve loose.

They always did say
Springfield is a wickeder town for women
than Chicago.
I see 'em on the streets.
It always was
an' I guess always will be.
Fifty per cent of the men that gets married

makes a mistake.
Why is that?

You're a white man
an' I'm a negro.
Your nationality don't make no difference.
    If I kill you
    Everybody says:
"Henry Stephens, a negro, killed a white man."
I got a little Indian blood in me
but that wouldn't count.

Springfield is Abraham Lincoln's town.
There's only eight mines out of twenty
In Sangamon county
Where the white miners
Let a negro work.

If I buy a house right next to the Peabody mine
That won't do no good.
Only white men digs coal there.
I got to walk a mile, two miles, further,
Where the black man can dig coal.
The United Mine Workers
Is one of the best or-gan-IZ-a-tions there is.
United means union,
And union means united.
But they's mines runnin' twenty-five years
And the white man never lets the negro in.

I remember when we was tryin' to organize.
We met in barns an' holes,
We met in the jungles.
I used to go to all the meetin's them days.
Now we meet downtown in a hall.

Now we's recognized by everybody
Fur one of the most powerful or-gan-IZ-a-tions
in the United States.
I don't go to meetin's nowadays
But if they's a cause to strike for I'll strike.
    I'd live in the fields on hard corn for a just cause.
Yes, for a just cause I'd live in the fields
On hard corn.

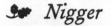 Nigger

I am the nigger.
Singer of songs,
Dancer . . .
Softer than fluff of cotton . . .
Harder than dark earth
Roads beaten in the sun
By the bare feet of slaves . . .
Foam of teeth . . . breaking crash of laughter . . .
Red love of the blood of woman,
White love of the tumbling pickaninnies . . .
Lazy love of the banjo thrum . . .
Sweated and driven for the harvest-wage,
Loud laughter with hands like hams,
Fists toughened on the handles,
Smiling the slumber dreams of old jungles,
Crazy as the sun and dew and dripping, heaving life of the jungle,
Brooding and muttering with memories of shackles:
        I am the nigger.
        Look at me.
        I am the nigger.

🐦 Man, the Man-Hunter

I saw Man, the man-hunter,
Hunting with a torch in one hand
And a kerosene can in the other,
Hunting with guns, ropes, shackles.

  I listened
  And the high cry rang.
The high cry of Man, the man-hunter:
We'll get you yet,   you   Son of a Bitch!

  I listened later,
  The high cry rang:
Kill him! kill him!   the Judean equivalent   the Son of a Bitch!

In the morning the sun saw
Two butts of something, a smoking rump,
And a warning in charred wood:
            Well, we got him,
            the   Son of a Bitch.

POET OF THE PEOPLE

Sandburg would become the Poet of the People Whitman had hoped to be, in large part because he encountered Whitman's work at a crucial time in his own journey toward creative identity and expression. Whitman gave him a model for social idealism, poetry, the life of the soul.

— PENELOPE NIVEN, from *Carl Sandburg: A Biography*

I Am the People, the Mob

I am the people—the mob—the crowd—the mass.

Do you know that all the great work of the world is done through me?

I am the workingman, the inventor, the maker of the world's food and clothes.

I am the audience that witnesses history. The Napoleons come from me and the Lincolns. They die. And then I send forth more Napoleons and Lincolns.

I am the seed ground. I am a prairie that will stand for much plowing. Terrible storms pass over me. I forget. The best of me is sucked out and wasted. I forget. Everything but Death comes to me and makes me work and give up what I have. And I forget.

Sometimes I growl, shake myself and spatter a few red drops for history to remember. Then—I forget.

When I, the People, learn to remember, when I, the People, use the lessons of yesterday and no longer forget who robbed me last year, who played me for a fool—then there will be no speaker in all the world say the name: "The People," with any fleck of a sneer in his voice or any far-off smile of derision.

The mob—the crowd—the mass—will arrive then.

🦋 A Reporter in Debt

The poet who kept himself in debt
knowing the big stream of people
live with their feet and shoulders
clambering through pits of debt,
the poet spoke easy:
"why should I be free who must write chains?
how shall I write chains unless the steel
clutches my wrists and ankles?
unless I am dirty and dusty from the pits
how can I write the people of the pits?"

🦋 My People

My people are gray,
    pigeon gray, dawn gray, storm gray.
I call them beautiful,
    and I wonder where they are going.

❧ *Poems Done on a Late Night Car*

I. CHICKENS

I am The Great White Way of the city:
When you ask what is my desire, I answer:
"Girls fresh as country wild flowers,
With young faces tired of the cows and barns,
Eager in their eyes as the dawn to find my mysteries,
Slender supple girls with shapely legs,
Lure in the arch of their little shoulders
And wisdom from the prairies to cry only softly at the ashes of my
    mysteries."

II. USED UP

*Lines based on certain regrets that come with rumination upon the
painted faces of women on North Clark Street, Chicago*

Roses,
Red roses,
Crushed
In the rain and wind
Like mouths of women
Beaten by the fists of
Men using them.
O little roses
And broken leaves
And petal wisps:
You that so flung your crimson

> To the sun
> Only yesterday.

III. HOME

Here is a thing my heart wishes the world had more of:
I heard it in the air of one night when I listened
To a mother singing softly to a child restless and angry in the
   darkness.

 *Prairie*

I was born on the prairie and the milk of its wheat, the red of its
   clover, the eyes of its women, gave me a song and a slogan.

Here the water went down, the icebergs slid with gravel, the gaps
   and the valleys hissed, and the black loam came, and the yellow
   sandy loam.
Here between the sheds of the Rocky Mountains and the Appalachi-
   ans, here now a morning star fixes a fire sign over the timber
   claims and cow pastures, the corn belt, the cotton belt, the cattle
   ranches.
Here the gray geese go five hundred miles and back with a wind
   under their wings honking the cry for a new home.
Here I know I will hanker after nothing so much as one more sunrise
   or a sky moon of fire doubled to a river moon of water.

The prairie sings to me in the forenoon and I know in the night I
   rest easy in the prairie arms, on the prairie heart.

   . . .

> After the sunburn of the day
> handling a pitchfork at a hayrack,

after the eggs and biscuit and coffee,
the pearl-gray haystacks
in the gloaming
are cool prayers
to the harvest hands.

In the city among the walls the overland passenger train is choked
and the pistons hiss and the wheels curse.
On the prairie the overland flits on phantom wheels and the sky and
the soil between them muffle the pistons and cheer the wheels.

. . .

I am here when the cities are gone.
I am here before the cities come.
I nourished the lonely men on horses.
I will keep the laughing men who ride iron.
I am dust of men.

The running water babbled to the deer, the cottontail, the gopher.
You came in wagons, making streets and schools,
Kin of the ax and rifle, kin of the plow and horse,
Singing *Yankee Doodle, Old Dan Tucker, Turkey in the Straw,*
You in the coonskin cap at a log house door hearing a lone wolf
howl,
You at a sod house door reading the blizzards and chinooks let loose
from Medicine Hat,
I am dust of your dust, as I am brother and mother
To the copper faces, the worker in flint and clay,
The singing women and their sons a thousand years ago
Marching single file the timber and the plain.

I hold the dust of these amid changing stars.
I last while old wars are fought, while peace broods mother-like,
While new wars arise and the fresh killings of young men.

I fed the boys who went to France in great dark days.
Appomattox is a beautiful word to me and so is Valley Forge and
    the Marne and Verdun,
I who have seen the red births and the red deaths
Of sons and daughters, I take peace or war, I say nothing and wait.

Have you seen a red sunset drip over one of my cornfields, the shore
    of night stars, the wave lines of dawn up a wheat valley?
Have you heard my threshing crews yelling in the chaff of a straw-
    pile and the running wheat of the wagonboards, my cornhuskers,
    my harvest hands hauling crops, singing dreams of women,
    worlds, horizons?

      . . .

          Rivers cut a path on flat lands.
          The mountains stand up.
          The salt oceans press in
          And push on the coast lines.
          The sun, the wind, bring rain
          And I know what the rainbow writes across the east or
             west in a half-circle:
          A love-letter pledge to come again.

      . . .

          Towns on the Soo Line,
          Towns on the Big Muddy,
          Laugh at each other for cubs
          And tease as children.

Omaha and Kansas City, Minneapolis and St. Paul, sisters in a house
    together, throwing slang, growing up.
Towns in the Ozarks, Dakota wheat towns, Wichita, Peoria, Buffalo,
    sisters throwing slang, growing up.

      . . .

Out of prairie-brown grass crossed with a streamer of wigwam
  smoke—out of a smoke pillar, a blue promise—out of wild
  ducks woven in greens and purples—
Here I saw a city rise and say to the peoples round the world: Listen,
  I am strong, I know what I want.
Out of log houses and stumps—canoes stripped from tree-sides—
  flatboats coaxed with an ax from the timber claims—in the years
  when the red and the white men met—the houses and streets rose.

A thousand red men cried and went away to new places for corn and
  women: a million white men came and put up skyscrapers, threw
  out rails and wires, feelers to the salt sea: now the smokestacks
  bite the skyline with stub teeth.

In an early year the call of a wild duck woven in greens and purples:
  now the riveter's chatter, the police patrol, the song-whistle of
  the steamboat.

To a man across a thousand years I offer a handshake.
I say to him: Brother, make the story short, for the stretch of a
  thousand years is short.

                    . . .

What brothers these in the dark?
What eaves of skyscrapers against a smoke moon?
These chimneys shaking on the lumber shanties
When the coal boats plow by on the river—
The hunched shoulders of the grain elevators—
The flame sprockets of the sheet steel mills
And the men in the rolling mills with their shirts off
Playing their flesh arms against the twisting wrists of steel:
                    what brothers these
                    in the dark
                    of a thousand years?

                    . . .

A headlight searches a snowstorm.

A funnel of white light shoots from over the pilot of the Pioneer Limited crossing Wisconsin.

In the morning hours, in the dawn,
The sun puts out the stars of the sky
And the headlight of the Limited train.

The fireman waves his hand to a country school teacher on a bobsled.

A boy, yellow hair, red scarf and mittens, on the bobsled, in his lunch box a pork chop sandwich and a V of gooseberry pie.

The horses fathom a snow to their knees.
Snow hats are on the rolling prairie hills.
The Mississippi bluffs wear snow hats.

   . . .

Keep your hogs on changing corn and mashes of grain,
    O farmerman.
    Cram their insides till they waddle on short legs
    Under the drums of bellies, hams of fat.
    Kill your hogs with a knife slit under the ear.
    Hack them with cleavers.
    Hang them with hooks in the hind legs.

   . . .

A wagonload of radishes on a summer morning.
Sprinkles of dew on the crimson-purple balls.
The farmer on the seat dangles the reins on the rumps of dapple-gray horses.
The farmer's daughter with a basket of eggs dreams of a new hat to wear to the county fair.

   . . .

On the left- and right-hand side of the road,

        Marching corn—

I saw it knee high weeks ago—now it is head high—tassels of red silk creep at the ends of the ears.

   • • •

I am the prairie, mother of men, waiting.

They are mine, the threshing crews eating beefsteak, the farmboys driving steers to the railroad cattle pens.

They are mine, the crowds of people at a Fourth of July basket picnic, listening to a lawyer read the Declaration of Independence, watching the pinwheels and Roman candles at night, the young men and women two by two hunting the bypaths and kissing-bridges.

They are mine, the horses looking over a fence in the frost of late October saying good morning to the horses hauling wagons of rutabaga to market.

They are mine, the old zigzag rail fences, the new barbwire.

   • • •

The cornhuskers wear leather on their hands.

There is no let-up to the wind.

Blue bandanas are knotted at the ruddy chins.

Falltime and winter apples take on the smolder of the five-o'clock November sunset: falltime, leaves, bonfires, stubble, the old things go, and the earth is grizzled.

The land and the people hold memories, even among the anthills and the angleworms, among the toads and woodroaches— among gravestone writings rubbed out by the rain—they keep old things that never grow old.

The frost loosens cornhusks.

The sun, the rain, the wind

        loosen cornhusks.

The men and women are helpers.
They are all cornhuskers together.
I see them late in the western evening
                in a smoke-red dust.

                . . .

The phantom of a yellow rooster flaunting a scarlet comb, on top of
    a dung pile crying hallelujah to the streaks of daylight,
The phantom of an old hunting dog nosing in the underbrush for
    muskrats, barking at a coon in a treetop at midnight, chewing a
    bone, chasing his tail round a corncrib,
The phantom of an old workhorse taking the steel point of a plow
    across a forty-acre field in spring, hitched to a harrow in summer,
    hitched to a wagon among cornshocks in fall,
These phantoms come into the talk and wonder of people on the
    front porch of a farmhouse late summer nights.
"The shapes that are gone are here," said an old man with a cob
    pipe in his teeth one night in Kansas with a hot wind on the
    alfalfa.

                . . .

Look at six eggs
In a mockingbird's nest.

Listen to six mockingbirds
Flinging follies of O-be-joyful
Over the marshes and uplands.

Look at songs
Hidden in eggs.

                . . .

When the morning sun is on the trumpet-vine blossoms, sing at the
    kitchen pans: Shout All Over God's Heaven.

When the rain slants on the potato hills and the sun plays a silver shaft on the last shower, sing to the bush at the backyard fence: Mighty Lak a Rose.

When the icy sleet pounds on the storm windows and the house lifts to a great breath, sing for the outside hills: The Ole Sheep Done Know the Road, the Young Lambs Must Find the Way.

. . .

Spring slips back with a girl face calling always: "Any new songs for me? Any new songs?"

O prairie girl, be lonely, singing, dreaming, waiting—your lover comes—your child comes—the years creep with toes of April rain on new-turned sod.

O prairie girl, whoever leaves you only crimson poppies to talk with, whoever puts a good-by kiss on your lips and never comes back—

There is a song deep as the falltime redhaws, long as the layer of black loam we go to, the shine of the morning star over the corn belt, the wave line of dawn up a wheat valley.

. . .

O prairie mother, I am one of your boys.

I have loved the prairie as a man with a heart shot full of pain over love.

Here I know I will hanker after nothing so much as one more sunrise or a sky moon of fire doubled to a river moon of water.

. . .

I speak of new cities and new people.

I tell you the past is a bucket of ashes.

I tell you yesterday is a wind gone down,
     a sun dropped in the west.

I tell you there is nothing in the world
  only an ocean of tomorrows,
  a sky of tomorrows.

I am a brother of the cornhuskers who say
  at sundown:
              Tomorrow is a day.

🌿 Cartoon

I am making a Cartoon of a Woman. She is the People. She is the
  Great Dirty Mother.
And Many Children hang on her Apron, crawl at her Feet, snuggle
  at her Breasts.

🌿 Smoke and Steel

Smoke of the fields in spring is one,
Smoke of the leaves in autumn another.
Smoke of a steel-mill roof or a battleship funnel,
They all go up in a line with a smokestack,
Or they twist . . . in the slow twist . . . of the wind.

If the north wind comes they run to the south.
If the west wind comes they run to the east.
      By this sign
      all smokes
      know each other.
Smoke of the fields in spring and leaves in autumn,

Smoke of the finished steel, chilled and blue,
By the oath of work they swear: "I know you."

Hunted and hissed from the center
Deep down long ago when God made us over,
Deep down are the cinders we came from—
You and I and our heads of smoke.

. . .

Some of the smokes God dropped on the job
Cross on the sky and count our years
And sing in the secrets of our numbers;
Sing their dawns and sing their evenings,
Sing an old log-fire song:

You may put the damper up,
You may put the damper down,
The smoke goes up the chimney just the same.
Smoke of a city sunset skyline,
Smoke of a country dusk horizon—
They cross on the sky and count our years.

. . .

Smoke of a brick-red dust
Winds on a spiral
Out of the stacks
For a hidden and glimpsing moon.
This, said the bar-iron shed to the blooming mill,
This is the slang of coal and steel.
The day-gang hands it to the night-gang,
The night-gang hands it back.

Stammer at the slang of this—
Let us understand half of it.
In the rolling mills and sheet mills,
In the harr and boom of the blast fires,

The smoke changes its shadow
And men change their shadow;
A nigger, a wop, a bohunk changes.

A bar of steel—it is only
Smoke at the heart of it, smoke and the blood of a man.
A runner of fire ran in it, ran out, ran somewhere else,
And left—smoke and the blood of a man
And the finished steel, chilled and blue.
So fire runs in, runs out, runs somewhere else again,
And the bar of steel is a gun, a wheel, a nail, a shovel,
A rudder under the sea, a steering-gear in the sky;
And always dark in the heart and through it,
        Smoke and the blood of a man.
Pittsburgh, Youngstown, Gary—they make their steel with men.

In the blood of men and the ink of chimneys
The smoke nights write their oaths:
Smoke into steel and blood into steel;
Homestead, Braddock, Birmingham, they make their steel with
        men.
Smoke and blood is the mix of steel.
        The birdmen drone
        in the blue; it is steel
        a motor sings and zooms.

        . . .

Steel barbwire around The Works.
Steel guns in the holsters of the guards at the gates of The Works.
Steel ore-boats bring the loads clawed from the earth by steel, lifted
        and lugged by arms of steel, sung on its way by the clanking
        clam-shells.

The runners now, the handlers now, are steel; they dig and clutch and haul; they hoist their automatic knuckles from job to job; they are steel making steel.

Fire and dust and air fight in the furnaces; the pour is timed, the billets wriggle; the clinkers are dumped:

Liners on the sea, skyscrapers on the land; diving steel in the sea, climbing steel in the sky.

   . . .

Finders in the dark, you Steve with a dinner bucket, you Steve clumping in the dusk on the sidewalks with an evening paper for the woman and kids, you Steve with your head wondering where we all end up—

Finders in the dark, Steve: I hook my arm in cinder sleeves; we go down the street together; it is all the same to us; you Steve and the rest of us end on the same stars; we all wear a hat in hell together, in hell or heaven.

Smoke nights now, Steve.
Smoke, smoke, lost in the sieves of yesterday;
Dumped again to the scoops and hooks today.
Smoke like the clocks and whistles, always.
    Smoke nights now.
    Tomorrow something else.

   . . .

Luck moons come and go:
Five men swim in a pot of red steel.
Their bones are kneaded into the bread of steel:
Their bones are knocked into coils and anvils
And the sucking plungers of sea-fighting turbines.
Look for them in the woven frame of a wireless station.
So ghosts hide in steel like heavy-armed men in mirrors.

Peepers, skulkers—they shadow-dance in laughing tombs.
They are always there and they never answer.

One of them said: "I like my job, the company is good to me,
America is a wonderful country."
One: "Jesus, my bones ache; the company is a liar; this is a free
country, like hell."
One: "I got a girl, a peach; we save up and go on a farm and raise
pigs and be the boss ourselves."
And the others were roughneck singers a long ways from home.
Look for them back of a steel vault door.

    They laugh at the cost.
    They lift the birdmen into the blue.
    It is steel a motor sings and zooms.

In the subway plugs and drums,
In the slow hydraulic drills, in gumbo or gravel,
Under dynamo shafts in the webs of armature spiders.
They shadow-dance and laugh at the cost.

    . . .

The ovens light a red dome.
Spools of fire wind and wind.
Quadrangles of crimson sputter.
The lashes of dying maroon let down.
Fire and wind wash out the slag.
Forever the slag gets washed in fire and wind.
The anthem learned by the steel is:
    Do this or go hungry.
Look for our rust on a plow.
Listen to us in a threshing-engine razz.
Look at our job in the running wagon wheat.

    . . .

Fire and wind wash at the slag.

Box-cars, clocks, steam-shovels, churns, pistons, boilers, scissors—

Oh, the sleeping slag from the mountains, the slag-heavy pig-iron will go down many roads.

Men will stab and shoot with it, and make butter and tunnel rivers, and mow hay in swaths, and slit hogs and skin beeves, and steer airplanes across North America, Europe, Asia, round the world.

Hacked from a hard rock country, broken and baked in mills and smelters, the rusty dust waits

Till the clean hard weave of its atoms cripples and blunts the drills chewing a hole in it.

The steel of its plinths and flanges is reckoned, O God, in one-millionth of an inch.

. . .

Once when I saw the curves of fire, the rough scarf women dancing,

Dancing out of the flues and smokestacks—flying hair of fire, flying feet upside down;

Buckets and baskets of fire exploding and chortling, fire running wild out of the steady and fastened ovens;

Sparks cracking a harr-harr-huff from a solar-plexus of rock-ribs of the earth taking a laugh for themselves;

Ears and noses of fire, gibbering gorilla arms of fire, gold mud-pies, gold bird-wings, red jackets riding purple mules, scarlet autocrats tumbling from the humps of camels, assassinated czars straddling vermilion balloons;

I saw then the fires flash one by one: good-by: then smoke, smoke;

And in the screens the great sisters of night and cool stars, sitting women arranging their hair,

Waiting in the sky, waiting with slow easy eyes, waiting and half-murmuring:

"Since you know all
and I know nothing,
tell me what I dreamed last night."
. . .

Pearl cobwebs in the windy rain,
in only a flicker of wind,
are caught and lost and never known again.

A pool of moonshine comes and waits,
but never waits long: the wind picks up
loose gold like this and is gone.

A bar of steel sleeps and looks slant-eyed
on the pearl cobwebs, the pools of moonshine;
sleeps slant-eyed a million years,
sleeps with a coat of rust, a vest of moths,
a shirt of gathering sod and loam.
The wind never bothers . . . a bar of steel.
The wind picks only . . . pearl cobwebs . . . pools of moonshine.

❧ *The Lawyers Know Too Much*

The lawyers, Bob, know too much.
They are chums of the books of old John Marshall.
They know it all, what a dead hand wrote,
A stiff dead hand and its knuckles crumbling,
The bones of the fingers a thin white ash.
    The lawyers know
    a dead man's thoughts too well.

In the heels of the higgling lawyers, Bob,
Too many slippery ifs and buts and howevers,

Too much hereinbefore provided whereas,
Too many doors to go in and out of.

> When the lawyers are through
> What is there left, Bob?
> Can a mouse nibble at it
> And find enough to fasten a tooth in?

> Why is there always a secret singing
> When a lawyer cashes in?
> Why does a hearse horse snicker
> Hauling a lawyer away?

The work of a bricklayer goes to the blue.
The knack of a mason outlasts a moon.
The hands of a plasterer hold a room together.
The land of a farmer wishes him back again.
> Singers of songs and dreamers of plays
> Build a house no wind blows over.
The lawyers—tell me why a hearse horse snickers hauling a
  lawyer's bones.

The Liars

(March, 1919)

A liar goes in fine clothes.
A liar goes in rags.
A liar is a liar, clothes or no clothes.
A liar is a liar and lives on the lies he tells
      and dies in a life of lies.

And the stonecutters earn a living—with lies—
        on the tombs of liars.

A liar looks 'em in the eye
And lies to a woman,
Lies to a man, a pal, a child, a fool.
And he is an old liar; we know him many years back.

  A liar to nations.
  A liar lies to the people.
A liar takes the blood of the people
And drinks this blood with a laugh and a lie,
  A laugh in his neck,
  A lie in his mouth.
And this liar is an old one; we know him many years.
  He is straight as a dog's hind leg.
  He is straight as a corkscrew.
He is white as a black cat's foot at midnight.

The tongue of a man is tied on this,
On the liar who lies to nations,
The liar who lies to the people.
The tongue of a man is tied on this
And ends: To hell with 'em all.
        To hell with 'em all.

It's a song hard as a riveter's hammer,
  Hard as the sleep of a crummy hobo,
  Hard as the sleep of a lousy doughboy,
Twisted as a shell-shock idiot's gibber.
The liars met where the doors were locked.
They said to each other: Now for war.
The liars fixed it and told 'em: Go.

Across their tables they fixed it up,
Behind their doors away from the mob.
And the guns did a job that nicked off millions.
The guns blew seven million off the map,
The guns sent seven million west.
Seven million shoving up the daisies.
Across their tables they fixed it up,
        The liars who lie to nations.

And now
Out of the butcher's job
And the boneyard junk the maggots have cleaned,
    Where the jaws of skulls tell the jokes of war ghosts,
Out of this they are calling now: Let's go back where we were.
        Let us run the world again, us, us.
Where the doors are locked the liars say: Wait and we'll cash in again.

So I hear The People talk.
I hear them tell each other:
    Let the strong men be ready.
    Let the strong men watch.
    Let your wrists be cool and your head clear.
    Let the liars get their finish,
    The liars and their waiting game, waiting a day again
    To open the doors and tell us: War! get out to your war again.

So I hear The People tell each other:
    Look at today and tomorrow.
    Fix this clock that nicks off millions
    When The Liars say it's time.
    Take things in your own hands.
        To hell with 'em all,
    The liars who lie to nations,
    The liars who lie to The People.

🌺 *Threes*

I was a boy when I heard three red words
a thousand Frenchmen died in the streets
for: Liberty, Equality, Fraternity—I asked
why men die for words.

I was older; men with mustaches, sideburns,
lilacs, told me the high golden words are:
Mother, Home, and Heaven—other older men with
face decorations said: God, Duty, Immortality
—they sang these threes slow from deep lungs.

Years ticked off their say-so on the great clocks
of doom and damnation, soup and nuts: meteors flashed
their say-so: and out of great Russia came three
dusky syllables workmen took guns and went out to die
for: Bread, Peace, Land.

And I met a marine of the U.S.A., a leatherneck with a girl on his
knee for a memory in ports circling the earth and he said: Tell me
how to say three things and I always get by—gimme a plate of ham
and eggs—how much?—and—do you love me, kid?

🌿 Red-Headed Restaurant Cashier

Shake back your hair, O red-headed girl.

Let go your laughter and keep your two proud freckles on your
 chin.

Somewhere is a man looking for a red-headed girl and some day
 maybe he will look into your eyes for a restaurant cashier and
 find a lover, maybe.

Around and around go ten thousand men hunting a red-headed girl
 with two freckles on her chin.

I have seen them hunting, hunting.

    Shake back your hair; let go your laughter.

🌿 Lines Written for Gene Kelly to Dance To

Spring is when the grass turns green and glad.

Spring is when the new grass comes up and says, "Hey, hey! Hey,
 hey!"

Be dizzy now and turn your head upside down and see how the
 world looks upside down.

Be dizzy now and turn a cartwheel, and see the good earth through
 a cartwheel.

Tell your feet the alphabet.

Tell your feet the multiplication table.

Tell your feet where to go, and watch 'em go and come back.

Can you dance a question mark?
Can you dance an exclamation point?
Can you dance a couple of commas?
And bring it to a finish with a period?

Can you dance like the wind is pushing you?
Can you dance like you are pushing the wind?
Can you dance with slow wooden heels
  and then change to bright and singing silver heels?
Such nice feet, such good feet.

So long as grass grows and rivers run
Silver lakes like blue porcelain plates
Silver snakes of winding rivers.
You can see 'em on a map.

Why we got geography?
Because we go from place to place. Because the earth used to be flat and
  had four corners, and you could jump off from any of the corners.
But now the earth is not flat any more. Now it is round all over.
  Now it is a globe, a ball, round all over, and we would all fall off
  it and tumble away into space if it wasn't for the magnetic poles.
  And when you dance it is the North Pole or the South Pole pulling
  on your feet like magnets to keep your feet on the earth.
And that's why we got geography.
And it's nice to have it that way.

Why does duh Mississippi River wind and wind?
Why, dat's easy. She wind so she git where she wanna go.
Mississippi, Rappahannock, Punxatawney. Spell out their names with
  your heels.

Where duh towns uh Punxatawney and Mauk Chunk? Why, yeanh
  day's bof in Pennsylvan-ee-eye-ay.
  And dat's why we got geography.

Left foot, tweedle-dum—right foot tweedle-dee, here they go.

When Yankee Doodle come to town, wot wuz he a-ridin' on?
A buffalo? A elephant? A horse?
No, no, no, no. A pony it wuz, a pony.
That's right—
Giddi-ap, Giddi-ap, Giddi-ap, Giddi-ap.
Whoa! Whoa!

🌿 Slabs of the Sunburnt West

I

Into the night, into the blanket of night,
Into the night rain gods, the night luck gods,
Overland goes the overland passenger train.

  Stand up, sandstone slabs of red,
Tell the overland passengers who burnt you.

Tell 'em how the jacks and screws loosened you.
Tell 'em who shook you by the heels and stood you on your heads,
Who put the slow pink of sunset mist on your faces.

Panels of the cold gray open night,
Gates of the Great American Desert,
    Skies keeping the prayers of the wagon men,
    The riders with picks, shovels and guns,
On the old trail, the Santa Fé trail, the Raton pass
Panels, skies, gates, listen tonight while we send up our prayers on
        the Santa Fé trail.

(A colossal bastard frog
squats in stone.
Once he squawked.
Then he was frozen and
shut up forever.)

Into the night the overland passenger train,
Slabs of sandstone red sink to the sunset red,
Blankets of night cover 'em up.
Night rain gods, night luck gods, are looking on.

March on, processions.
Tie your hat to the saddle and ride, O Rider.
Let your ponies drag their navels in the sand.
Go hungry; leave your bones in the desert sand.
When the desert takes you the wind is clean.
The winds say so on a noisy night.
    The fingerbone of a man
    lay next to the handle of a frying pan
    and the footbone of a horse.
"Clean, we are clean," the winds whimper on a noisy night.

Into the night the overland passenger train,
And the engineer with an eye for signal lights,
And the porters making up berths for passengers,
And the boys in the diner locking the icebox—
And six men with cigars in the buffet car mention "civilization,"
    "history," "God."

Into the blanket of night goes the overland train,
Into the black of the night the processions march,
    The ghost of a pony goes by,
    A hat tied to the saddle,
    The wagon tongue of a prairie schooner
    And the handle of a Forty-niner's pickax

Do a shiver dance in the desert dust,
   In the coyote gray of the alkali dust.
And—six men with cigars in the buffet car mention "civilization,"
   "history," "God."

Sleep, O wonderful hungry people.
Take a shut-eye, take a long old snooze,
   and be good to yourselves;
Into the night the overland passenger train
And the sleepers cleared for a morning sun
   and the Grand Canyon of Arizona.

2

   A bluejay blue
   and a gray mouse gray
   ran up the canyon walls.

A rider came to the rim
Of a slash and a gap of desert dirt—
A long-legged long-headed rider
On a blunt and a blurry jackass—
Riding and asking, "How come? How come?"
And the long-legged long-headed rider said.
"Between two ears of a blurry jackass
I see ten miles of auburn, gold and purple—
I see doors open over doorsills
And always another door and a doorsill.
Cheat my eyes, fill me with the float
Of your dream, you auburn, gold, and purple.
Cheat me, blow me off my pins onto footless floors.
Let me put footsteps in an airpath.
Cheat me with footprints on auburn, gold, purple
Out to the last violet shimmer of the float

Of the dream—and I will come straddling a jackass,
Singing a song and letting out hallelujahs
To the doorsill of the last footprint."

And the man took a stub lead pencil
And made a long memo in shorthand
On the two blurry jackass ears:—

"God sits with long whiskers in the sky."
I said it when I was a boy.
I said it because long-whiskered men
Put it in my head to say it.
     They lied ... about you ... God ...
     They lied. ...

The other side of the five doors
and doorsills put in my house—
how many hinges, panels, doorknobs,
how many locks and lintels,
put on the doors and doorsills
winding and wild between
the first and the last doorsill of all?

"Out of the footprints on ten miles
of auburn, gold and purple—an old song comes:
These bones shall rise again,
Yes, children, these bones shall rise.

"Yonder past my five doors
are fifty million doors, maybe,
stars with knobs and locks and lintels,
stars with riders of rockets,
stars with swimmers of fire.

"Cheat my eyes—and I come again—
straddling a jackass—singing a song—
letting out hallelujahs.

"If God is a proud and a cunning Bricklayer,
Or if God is a King in a white gold Heaven,
Or if God is a Boss and a Watchman always watching,
I come riding the old ride of the humiliation,
Straddling a jackass, singing a song,
Letting out hallelujahs.

"Before a ten mile float
of auburn, gold, and purple,
footprints on a sunset airpath haze,
     I ask:
How can I taste with my tongue a tongueless God?
How can I touch with my fingers a fingerless God?
How can I hear with my ears an earless God?
Or smell of a God gone noseless long ago?
Or look on a God who never needs eyes for looking?

"My head is under your foot, God.
My head is a pan of alkali dust
your foot kicked loose—your foot of air
with its steps on the sunset airpath haze.

          (A bluejay blue
          and a gray mouse gray
          ran up the canyon walls.)

"Sitting at the rim of the big gap
at the high lash of the frozen storm line,
I ask why I go on five crutches,
tongues, ears, nostrils—all cripples—
eyes and nose—both cripples—

I ask why these five cripples
limp and squint and gag with me,
why they say with the oldest frozen faces:
    Man is a poor stick and a sad squirt;
    if he is poor he can't dress up;
    if he dresses up he don't know any place to go.

"Away and away on some green moon
a blind blue horse eats white grass
    And the blind blue horse knows more than I do
    because he saw more than I have seen
    and remembered it after he went blind.

"And away and away on some other green moon
is a sea-kept child who lacks a nose I got
and fingers like mine and all I have.
And yet the sea-kept child knows more than
I do and sings secrets alien to me as light
to a nosing mole underground.
I understand this child as a yellow-belly
catfish in China understands peach pickers
at sunrise in September in a Michigan orchard.

    "The power and lift of the sea
    and the flame of the old earth fires under,
I sift their meanings of sand in my fingers.
I send out five sleepwalkers to find out who I am,
    my name and number, where I came from,
    and where I am going.
They go out, look, listen, wonder, and shoot a fire-white rocket
    across the night sky; the shot and the flare of the rocket dies to a
    whisper; and the night is the same as it always was.
They come back, my five sleepwalkers; they have an answer for
    me, they say; they tell me: *Wait*—the password all of them

heard when the fire-white rocket shot across the sky and died to
a whisper, the password is: *Wait.*

"I sit with five binoculars, amplifiers, spectroscopes
I sit looking through five windows, listening, tasting, smelling,
    touching
I sit counting five million smoke fogs.
Repeaters, repeaters, come back to my window-sills.
Some are pigeons coming to coo and coo and clean their tail feathers
    and look wise at me.
Some are pigeons coming with broken wings to die with pain in
    their eyes on my window-sills.

"I walk the high lash of the frozen storm line;
I sit down with my feet in a ten-mile gravel pit.
Here I ask why I am a bag of sea-water fastened
to a frame of bones put walking on land—here I
look at crawlers, crimson, spiders spotted with
purple spots on their heads, flinging silver nets,
two, four, six, against the sun.
Here I look two miles down to the ditch of the sea
and pick a winding ribbon, a river eater, a water
grinder; it is a runner sent to run by a stop-watch,
it is a wrecker on a rush job."

> (A bluejay blue
> and a gray mouse gray
> ran up the canyon walls.)

Battering rams, blind mules, mounted policemen,
trucks hauling caverns of granite, elephants
grappling gorillas in a death strangle, cathedrals,
arenas, platforms, somersaults of telescoped rail-
road train wrecks, exhausted egg heads, piles of
skulls, mountains of empty sockets, mummies of kings

and mobs, memories of work gangs and wrecking crews,
sobs of wind and water storms, all frozen and held
on paths leading on to spirals of new zigzags—

An arm-chair for a one-eyed giant;
two pine trees grow in the left arm of the chair;
a bluejay comes, sits, goes, comes again;
a bluejay shoots and twitters . . . out and across . . .
tumbled skyscrapers and wrecked battleships,
walls of crucifixions and wedding breakfasts;
ruin, ruin—a brute gnashed, dug, kept on—
kept on and quit: and this is It.
Falling away, the brute is working.
Sheets of white veils cross a woman's face.
An eye socket glooms and wonders.
The brute hangs his head and drags on to the job.
The mother of mist and light and air murmurs: Wait.

The weavers of light weave best in red,
    better in blue.
The weavers of shadows weave at sunset;
    the young black-eyed women run, run, run
    to the night star homes; the old women
    sit weaving for the night rain gods,
    the night luck gods.

Eighteen old giants throw a red gold shadow ball;
they pass it along; hands go up and stop it; they
bat up flies and practice; they begin the game, they
knock it for home runs and two-baggers; the pitcher
put it across in an out- and an in-shoot drop; the
Devil is the Umpire; God is the Umpire; the game
is called on account of darkness.

A bluejay blue
and a gray mouse gray
ran up the canyon walls.

3

Good night; it is scribbled on the panels
of the cold gray open desert.
Good night; on the big sky blanket over the
Santa Fé trail it is woven in the oldest
Indian blanket songs.

Buffers of land, breakers of sea, say it and
say it, over and over, good night, good night.

    Tie your hat to the saddle
    and ride, ride, ride, O Rider.
    Lay your rails and wires
    and ride, ride, ride, O Rider.
The worn tired stars say
you shall die early and die dirty.
The clean cold stars say
you shall die late and die clean.

The runaway stars say
you shall never die at all,
never at all.

🌿 A Couple

He was in Cincinnati, she in Burlington.
He was in a gang of Postal Telegraph linemen.
She was a pot rassler in a boarding house.
"The crying is lonely," she wrote him.
"The same here," he answered.
The winter went by and he came back and they married
And he went away again where rainstorms knocked down
    telegraph poles and wires dropped with frozen sleet.
And again she wrote him, "The crying is lonely."
And again he answered, "The same here."
Their five children are in the public schools.
He votes the Republican ticket and is a taxpayer.
They are known among those who know them
As honest American citizens living honest lives.
Many things that bother other people never bother them.
They have their five children and they are a couple,
A pair of birds that call to each other and satisfy.
As sure as he goes away she writes him, "The crying is lonely"
And he flashes back the old answer, "The same here."
It is a long time since he was a gang lineman at Cincinnati
And she was a pot rassler in a Burlington boarding house;
Yet they never get tired of each other; they are a couple.

❧ The People, Yes

I

From the four corners of the earth,
from corners lashed in wind
and bitten with rain and fire,
from places where the winds begin
and fogs are born with mist children,
tall men from tall rocky slopes came
and sleepy men from sleepy valleys,
their women tall, their women sleepy,
with bundles and belongings,
with little ones babbling, "Where to now?
    what next?"

The people of the earth, the family of man,
wanted to put up something proud to look at,
a tower from the flat land of earth
on up through the ceiling into the top of the sky.

    And the big job got going,
    the caissons and pilings sunk,
    floors, walls and winding staircases
    aimed at the stars high over,
    aimed to go beyond the ladders of the moon.

    And God Almighty could have struck them dead
    or smitten them deaf and dumb.

And God was a whimsical fixer.
God was an understanding Boss
with another plan in mind,
And suddenly shuffled all the languages,
changed the tongues of men
so they all talked different
And the masons couldn't get what the hodcarriers said,
The helpers handed the carpenters the wrong tools,
Five hundred ways to say, "W h o   a r e   y o u ?"
Changed ways of asking, "Where do we go from here?"
Or of saying, "Being born is only the beginning,"
Or, "Would you just as soon sing as make that noise?"
Or, "What you don't know won't hurt you."
And the material-and-supply men started disputes
With the hauling gangs and the building trades
And the architects tore their hair over the blueprints
And the brickmakers and the mule skinners talked back
To the straw bosses who talked back to the superintendents
And the signals got mixed; the men who shovelled the bucket
Hooted the hoisting men—and the job was wrecked.

Some called it the Tower of Babel job
And the people gave it many other names.
The wreck of it stood as a skull and a ghost,
a memorandum hardly begun,
swaying and sagging in tall hostile winds,
held up by slow friendly winds.

4

The people know what the land knows
the numbers odd and even of the land
the slow hot wind of summer and its withering

or again the crimp of the driving white blizzard
and neither of them to be stopped
neither saying anything else than:
> "I'm not arguing. I'm telling you."

The old timer on the desert was gray
and grizzled with ever seeing the sun:
> "For myself I don't care whether it rains.
> I've seen it rain.
> But I'd like to have it rain
> pretty soon sometime.
> Then my son could see it.
> He's never seen it rain."

"Out here on the desert,"
> said the first woman who said it,
> > "the first year you don't believe
> > what others tell you
> > and the second year you don't
> > believe what you tell yourself."
"I weave thee, I weave thee,"
sang the weaving Sonora woman.
"I weave thee,
> thou art for a Sonora fool."

And the fool spoke of her,
over wine mentioned her:
"She can teach a pair of stilts to dance."

"What is the east? Have you been in the east?"
the New Jersey woman asked the little girl
the wee child growing up in Arizona who said:
"Yes, I've been in the east,
the east is where trees come
between you and the sky."

Another baby in Cleveland, Ohio,
in Cuyahoga County, Ohio—
why did she ask:
> "Papa
> what is the moon
> supposed to advertise?"

And the boy in Winnetka, Illinois who wanted to know:
"Is there a train so long you can't count the cars?
Is there a blackboard so long it will hold all the numbers?"

What of the Athenian last year on whose bosom
a committee hung a medal to say to the world
here is a champion heavyweight poet?
He stood on a two-masted schooner
and flung his medal far out on the sea bosom.
> "And why not?
> Has anybody ever given the ocean a medal?
> Who of the poets equals the music of the sea?
> And where is a symbol of the people
> > unless it is the sea?"

"Is it far to the next town?"
asked the Arkansas traveller
who was given the comfort:
> "It seems farther than it is
> but you'll find it ain't."

Six feet six was Davy Tipton
and he had the proportions
as kingpin Mississippi River pilot
nearly filling the pilothouse
as he took the wheel with a laugh:
"Big rivers ought to have big men."

On the homestretch of a racetrack
in the heart of the bluegrass country
in Lexington, Kentucky
they strewed the ashes of a man
who had so ordered in his will.

He loved horses
and wanted his dust
in the flying hoofs of the homestretch.

     20

Who shall speak for the people?
Who knows the works from A to Z
    so he can say, "I know what the
    people want"? Who is this phenom?
    where did he come from?
When have the people been halt as rotten
    as what the panderers to the people
    dangle before crowds?
When has the fiber of the people been as
    shoddy as what is sold to the people
    by cheaters?
What is it the panderers and cheaters of
    the people play with and trade on?
The credulity of believers and hopers—and
    when is a heart less of a heart because
    of belief and hope?
What is the tremulous line between credulity
    on the one side and on the other
    the hypotheses and illusions of inventors,
    discoverers, navigators who chart
    their course by what they hope and
    believe is beyond the horizon?

What is a stratosphere fourteen miles from
    the earth or a sunken glass house on
    the sea-bottom amid fish and feather-
    stars unless a bet that man can shove
    on beyond yesterday's record of man
    the hoper, the believer?
How like a sublime sanctuary of human
    credulity is that room where amid
    tubes, globes and retorts they shoot
    with heavy hearts of hydrogen and
    batter with fire-streams of power
    hoping to smash the atom:
Who are these bipeds trying to take apart
    the atom and isolate its electrons and
    make it tell why it is what it is?
    Believers and hopers.
Let the work of their fathers and elder
    brothers be cancelled this instant and
    what would happen?
Nothing—only every tool, bus, car, light,
    torch, bulb, print, film, instrument or
    communication depending for its life
    on electrodynamic power would stop
    and stand dumb and silent.

        3 7

"So you want to divide all the money there is
    and give every man his share?"
"That's it. Put it all in one big pile and split
it even for everybody."
"And the land, the gold, silver, oil, copper, you want
that divided up?"

"Sure—an even whack for all of us."
"Do you mean that to go for horses and cows?"
"Sure—why not?"
"And how about pigs?"
"Oh to hell with you—you know I got a couple of
pigs."

In the night and the mist these voices:
What is mine is mine and I am going to keep it.
What is yours is yours and you are welcome to keep it.
You will have to fight me to take from me what is mine.
Part of what is mine is yours and you are welcome to it.
What is yours is mine and I am going to take it from you.
      In the night and the mist
      the voices meet
      as the clash of steel on steel
Over the rights of possession and control and the points:
      what is mine? what is yours?
      and who says so?

The poor were divided into
the deserving and the undeserving
and a pioneer San Franciscan lacked words:
"It's hard enough to be poor
but to be poor and undeserving . . ."
He saw the slumborn illborn wearyborn
from fathers and mothers the same
out of rooms dank with rot
and scabs, rags, festerings, tubercles, chancres,
the very doorways quavering,
"What's the use?"

"I came to a country,"
said a wind-bitten vagabond,

"where I saw shoemakers barefoot
saying they had made too many shoes.
I met carpenters living outdoors
saying they had built too many houses.
Clothing workers I talked with,
bushelmen and armhole-basters,
said their coats were on a ragged edge
because they had made too many coats.
And I talked with farmers, yeomanry,
the backbone of the country,
so they were told,
saying they were in debt and near starvation
because they had gone ahead like always
and raised too much wheat and corn
too many hogs, sheep, cattle.
When I said, 'You live in a strange country,'
they answered slow, like men
who wouldn't waste anything, not even language:
'You ain't far wrong there, young feller.
We're going to do something, we don't know what.'"

    The drowning man in the river
    answered the man on the bridge:
    "I don't want to die,
    I'll lose my job in the molding room of
    the Malleable Iron and Castings Works."
    And the living man on the bridge
    hotfooted to the molding room foreman
    of the Malleable Iron and Castings Works
    and got a short answer:
    "You're ten minutes late. The man who
    pushed that fellow off the bridge
    is already on the job."

"What do you want?" a passing stranger asked
a County Kerry farmer.
"What is it I'm wantin'? Me byes and girruls
is gone. The rain has rotted the prathies.
The landlord has taken me pig for the rint.
All I'm wantin' is the Judgment Day."

"The poor of the earth hide themselves together," wrote Job mean-
ing in those days too they had a shantytown.
"As wild asses in the wilderness they must go forth, to seek food as
their task," wrote Job meaning then too they carried the banner
and hoped to connect with board and clothes somehow.
"In a field not theirs they harvest," wrote Job as though in Judea
then the frontier was gone, as now in America instead of free
homesteads the signs say: No Trespassing.
"The weaklings groan and the souls of the wounded cry for help,"
wrote Job taking special notice of those "forced to garner the
vineyard of the wicked one," mentioning footless wanderers of
Bible times as though the devices of men then too had an edge
against the propertyless.

In the Sunflower State 1928 Anno Domini
a Jayhawker sunburnt and gaunt
drove to a loading platform
and took what he got for his hogs
and spoke before two other hog raisers:
        "Everything's lopsided.
"I raise hogs and the railroads and the banks take them away from
me and I get hit in the hind end.
"The more hogs I raise the worse my mortgages look.
"I try to sleep and I hear those mortgages gnawing in the night like
rats in a corn crib.
"I want to shoot somebody but I don't know who.
"We'll do something. You wait and see.

"We don't have to stand for this skin game if we're free
  Americans."

        "Get off this estate."
        "What for?"
        "Because it's mine."
        "Where did you get it?"
        "From my father."
        "Where did he get it?"
        "From his father."
        "And where did he get it?"
        "He fought for it."
        "Well, I'll fight you for it."

    58

      The people, yes,
      Out of what is their change
      from chaos to order
      and chaos again?

"Yours till the hangman doth us part,"
Don Magregor ended his letters.

"It annoys me to die,"
said a philosopher.
"I should like to see what follows."

To those who had ordered them to death,
one of them said:
    "We die because the people are asleep
    and you will die because the people will awaken."

Greek met Greek when Phocion and Democritus spoke.
"You will drive the Athenians mad some day and they will kill
    you."

"Yes, me when they go mad, and as sure as they get sane again,
you."

7 8

What did Hiamovi, the red man, Chief of
the Cheyennes, have?
To a great chief at Washington and to a
chief of peoples across the waters,
Hiamovi spoke:
"There are birds of many colors—red, blue,
green, yellow,
Yet it is all one bird.
There are horses of many colors—brown,
black, yellow, white,
Yet it is all one horse.
So cattle, so all living things, animals,
flowers, trees.
So men in this land, where once were only
Indians, are now men of many colors—
white, black, yellow, red.
Yet all one people.
That this should come to pass was in the
heart of the Great Mystery.
It is right thus—and everywhere there
shall be peace."
Thus Hiamovi, out of a tarnished and weather-
worn heart of old gold, out of a living
dawn gold.

What is the float of life that goes by us
in certain moods of autumn smoke
when tall trees seem in the possession of phantoms
carrying a scheme of haze

inevitably past changing sunsets
into a moist moonlight
and beyond into a baffling moonset
on a mist horizon?
These devices are made of what color and air?
And how far and in how does man make them himself?
    What is this pool of reverie
    this blur of contemplation
    wherein man is brother to mud and gold
    to bug and bird
    to behemoths and constellations?

In the evening twilight in the skyscraper office
and the hoom hoom of a big steamboat docking
and the auto horns and the corner newboys
only half heard as far up as sixteen floors
the doctor meditated and spoke: "The rich come afraid to die, afraid
to have their throats looked into, their intestines prodded. It
hurts. Their power of resistance is gone. They can't stand pain.
Things go wrong, they come into my office and ask what is the
matter. I have to be careful how I say, 'You are growing old, that
is all, everybody grows old, we all have to die.' That scares them.
They don't want to grow old. They tell me I must find a way to
keep them from growing old. They don't want to die. They tell
me they will pay me to find a way so they won't have to die."
Thus in the evening twilight, in the hoom hoom and the auto
horns and the corner newsboys only half heard up sixteen floors.
    And he went on:
"I was in a hospital the other day. A man blind thirty-five years
could see again. We walked out together. And up the street he
saw a horse. He asked, 'What is that?' I said, 'It's a horse—
didn't you ever see a horse before?' He answered, 'No, this is the
first time I ever saw a horse.'"

Thus in the evening twilight
in the hoom hoom.

And the doctor went on: "A few weeks ago came a woman saying
she had been to a great symphony concert, going out to walk
miles, still hearing the grand crashes of that music, walking home
on air, telling me, 'I went to bed and wept for three weeks—
what is the matter with me?' I had to tell her, 'Only a slight
matter. You will be well again when you learn to listen to the
ticking of the clock.'"
To a lawyer who came saying he had undertaken more financial
reorganizations than there was time for and his nerves were shot
the doctor talked long about worry, gave the lawyer a box and
100 black beans: "Each morning you drop a bean in the box and
say, 'Worry is in the bean and the bean is in the box.'"
In the hoom hoom of the big steamboat docking the doctor said,
"Silence is the great gratitude when bad music ends."

        1 0 7

        The people will live on.
The learning and blundering people will live on.
        They will be tricked and sold and again sold
And go back to the nourishing earth for rootholds,
        The people so peculiar in renewal and comeback,
        You can't laugh off their capacity to take it.
The mammoth rests between his cyclonic dramas.

The people so often sleepy, weary, enigmatic,
is a vast huddle with many units saying:
        "I earn my living.
        I make enough to get by
        and it takes all my time.
        If I had more time

I could do more for myself
and maybe for others.
I could read and study
and talk things over
and find out about things.
It takes time.
I wish I had the time."
The people is a tragic and comic two-face:
hero and hoodlum: phantom and gorilla twist-
ing to moan with a gargoyle mouth: "They
buy me and sell me . . . it's a game . . .
sometime I'll break loose . . ."

    Once having marched
Over the margins of animal necessity,
Over the grim line of sheer subsistence
    Then man came
To the deeper rituals of his bones,
To the lights lighter than any bones,
To the time for thinking things over,
To the dance, the song, the story,
Or the hours given over to dreaming,
    Once having so marched.

Between the finite limitations of the five senses
and the endless yearnings of man for the beyond
the people hold to the humdrum bidding of work and food
while reaching out when it comes their way
for lights beyond the prisms of the five senses,
for keepsakes lasting beyond any hunger or death.
    This reaching is alive.
The panderers and liars have violated and smutted it.
    Yet this reaching is alive yet
    for lights and keepsakes.

The people know the salt of the sea
and the strength of the winds
lashing the corners of the earth.
The people take the earth
as a tomb of rest and a cradle of hope.
Who else speaks for the Family of Man?
They are in tune and step
with constellations of universal law.

The people is a polychrome,
a spectrum and a prism
held in a moving monolith,
a console organ of changing themes,
a clavilux of color poems
wherein the sea offers fog
and the fog moves off in rain
and the labrador sunset shortens
to a nocturne of clear stars
serene over the shot spray
of northern lights.

The steel mill sky is alive.
The fire breaks white and zigzag
shot on a gun-metal gloaming.
Man is a long time coming.
Man will yet win.
Brother may yet line up with brother:

This old anvil laughs at many broken hammers.
There are men who can't be bought.
The fireborn are at home in fire.
The stars make no noise.
You can't hinder the wind from blowing.

Time is a great teacher.
Who can live without hope?

In the darkness with a great bundle of grief
    the people march.
In the night, and overhead a shovel of stars for
    keeps, the people march:
                    "Where to? what next?"

🌿 *Timesweep*

I was born in the morning of the world,
So I know how morning looks,
    morning in the valley wanting,
    morning on a mountain wanting.
Morning looks like people look,
    like a cornfield wanting corn,
    like a sea wanting ships.
Tell me about any strong beautiful wanting
    And there is your morning, my morning,
                everybody's morning.

Makers and givers may be moon shaken,
                may be star lost,
Knowing themselves as sea-deep seekers,
                both seeking and sought,
Knowing love is a ring and the ring endless,
Seeing love as a wheel and the wheel endless.

    Love may be a hard flesh crying its want.
    Love may be a thin horizon air,
        thinner than snowwhite wool finespun,

finer than any faint blue mist
blown away and gone on yesterday's wind.

> There are hungers
> for a nameless bread
> out of the dust
> of the hard earth,
> out of the blaze
> of the calm sun.

Blow now, winds, you so old at blowing.
Oak at the river, pine at the rocks,
    brandish your arms
Slow to a whisper wind, fast to a storm howl.

. . .

The wind carves sand into shapes,
Endless the fresh designs,
Wind and ice patient beyond telling.
Ice can tip mountains over,
Ice the giant beyond measure.
And the sun governs valley lights,
Transforms hats into shoes and back again
Before we are through any long looking.

. . .

The pink nipples of the earth in springtime,
The long black eyelashes of summer's look,
The harvest laughter of tawny autumn,
The winter silence of land in snow covers,
Each speaks its own oaths of the cool and the flame
of naked possessions clothed and come naked again:
        The sea knows it all.
        They all crept out of the sea.

. . .

These wheels within wheels
These leaves folded in leaves
These wheeling winds
   and winding leaves
Those sprockets
   from those seeds
This spiral shooting
   from that rainfall—
What does a turning earth
   say to its axis?
How should a melon say thanks
Or a squash utter blessings?
   . . .

In the heave of the hankering sea
God put precisions of music and accord
to be heard in the deepest seabells
amid the farthest violet spawn
moving in seagreen doom and skyblue promise.
   The sea shares its tokens—
     how and with whom?

To these shores birds return
   and keep returning
for the curves of fresh flights.
To these waters fish return
   and keep returning
for the fathoming of old waters.
To sky and sea they are born
and keep returning to be reborn.

The sharing of the sea goes on
for the sake of wings and fins

ever returning to new skyblue,
ever reborn in new seagreen.

Could the gray-green lobster speak
  what would he say
  of personal secrets?
Could one white gull utter a word—
  what would it be?
  what white feather of a word?

          . . .

Among the shapes and shadow-shapes
in the blurs of the marching animals,
among the open forms, the hidden and half-hidden,
  who is the Head One? Me? Man?
  Am I first over all, I the genus homo?

  Where did I come from?
  How doing now and where to from here?
  Is there any going back?
  And where might I want to go back?
Is it told in my dreams and hankerings, looking
  back at what I was, seeing what I am?
  Like so a man talking to himself
  of the bitter, the sweet, the bittersweet:
  he had heard likenings of himself:
Cock of the walk, brave as a lion, fierce as a tiger,
Stubborn as a mule, mean as a louse, crazy as a bedbug,
Soft as a kitten, slimy as an octopus, one poor fish.

  Then he spoke for himself:
  I am bat-eyed, chicken-hearted, monkey-faced.
  Listen and you'll hear it told,
  I am a beast out of the jungle.
  Man, proud man, with a peacock strut

seeing himself in his own man-made mirrors.
    Yet I am myself all the animals.
Mix in among lavender shadows the gorilla far back
And the jungle cry of readiness for death
Or struggle—and the clean breeds who live on
In the underbrush. Mix in farther back yet
Breeds out of the slime of the sea.
Put in a high green of a restless sea.
Insinuate chlorine and mystic salts,
The make-up of vertebrates,
the long highway of mammals who chew
Their victims and feed their children
From milk at a breast,
The fathers and the mothers who battled hunger
And tore each other's jugulars
Over land and women, laughter and language.
Put in mystery without end. Then add mystery.
    The memorandum runs long.
    I have feet, fins and wings.
    I live on land, in the sea, in the air.
    I run, fly, sneak, prowl, I kill and eat.
    Among killers and eaters I am first.
    I am the Head One.

What is this load I carry out of yesterday?
What are the bygones of dreams, moans, shadows?
What jargons, what gibberish, must I yet unlearn?
I have been a dim plasm in the sea,
rocking dumb, not-so-dumb, dumb again,
    a dab and a dangling tangle
    swarming and splitting to live again.

I have been a drop of jelly
    aching with a silver shot of light
        and it sang Be-now Now-be Be-now Now-be.

I have been a rockabye baby
sloshed in the sludge of the sea
and I have clung with a shell over me
waiting a tide to bring me breakfast.

I have been the little fish eaten by the big one
and I have been the big fish
taking ten lesser fish in one fast gulp.

I have been a shrimp, one of a billion,
fed to a million little fish
ending as fodder in the bellies of big fish.
In the seven seas
of the one vast glumbering sea over the globe
I have been eater and eaten,
toiler and hanger-on.

I lived half in the sea, half on land,
swimmer and crawler, fins and legs.

I traveled with layers of earthworms
grinding limestone into loam.

Encased as a snail
I wrought one pure spiral,
an image of no beginning, no end.
"This is the image wherein I live;
the outer form of me to be here
when the dried inner one drifts
away into thin air."
I have journeyed

for sticks and mud and weaving thongs
to build me a home in a bush.

I have mounted into the blue sky
with a mate lark on a summer morning,
dropping into sycamore branches to warble.

The orioles called me one of theirs;
herons taught me to stand and wait in marsh grass,
to preen my wings and rise with legs bundled behind.

    I was the awkward pelican
    flying low along the florida coast with a baby.

    I stood with pink flamingoes
    in long lagoons at tallahassee watching sunrise.

I am black as a crow with a *caw-caw* in my throat
and I am lush with morning calls of catbird and mocker,
the cardinal's *what-cheer what-cheer*
and the redbird's whistle across hemlock timbers
in early april in wisconsin.

I have done the cleansing service
of scavengers on land and sea;
the red and sea-green lobsters told me
how they win a living.
I have slunk among buzzards and broken hunger
with a beak in a rottening horse.
I have fed where my greatgrandfathers fed.

I know the faint half-words
of the fly and the flea,
the midge, the mosquito.
I was kin of a vampire
doing what a blind thirst told me.

A louse seeking red blood told me
I carry feeders in blood.
I ganged up with maggots
and cleaned a cadaver
and left the bones gleaming.

I am a grasshopper taking in one jump
a hundred grasshopper lengths.
I buzz with earnest bees
in the lingering sun of apple orchards.
I loiter with tumble bugs
seeming to know solemn causes.
I climb with spiders, throw ladders, nets,
frameworks out of my navel coils.
I am the building ant
of architectonic galleries and chambers.
I am egg, cocoon and moth.
I count my caterpillar rings of black and yellow.
I inch with the inch worms
measuring pearl-green miles of summer months.
I have swept in the ashen paths of weevils,
borers, chinch bugs eating their way.
Born once as a late morning child
I died of old age before noon.
Or again I issued as a luna moth,
circles of gold spotting my lavender wings.
I have zigzagged with blue water bugs
among white lotus and pond lilies.
From my silver throat in the dew of evening
came a whippoorwill call, one, another, more
as a slow gold moon told time with climbing.

I am the chameleon taking the tint of what I live on,
the water frog green as the scum he sits on,
the tree frog gray as the tree-bark-gray.
The duck, the swan, the goose, met me as sisters,
the beaver, the porcupine, the chinchilla, as brothers.
The rattlesnakes let me live with them
to eat mice, to salivate birds and rabbits
and fatten in sleep on noontime rocks.
I was a lizard, a texas horned toad,
a centipede counting my century of legs.
I was a crocodile in africa
with a lazy mouthful of teeth.

The stealth of the rat, the mink, the squirrel, came.
The weasel gave me his lingo
of now-you-see-me now-you-don't.
The rabbit hide-out in clover, the gopher hole,
the mole tunnel, the corn-shock nest of the mouse,
these were a few of my homes.
One summer night with fireflies
I too was fluttering night gold.

Long ago I ran with the eohippus,
the little horse that was.
I wore dodo feathers
but that's all passed.
I had a feathered form fade in fog:
you can find it now in feathered fossils.
I was a mammoth, a dinosaur
and other hulks too big to last.
I have been more quadrupeds than I can name.
I was the son of a wild jackass
with swift and punishing heels.
I lifted my legs and carried a camel hump

in slow caravans pausing at nightfall,
lifting my hump again at dawn.

I locked my horns with another moose;
our antlers lie locked and our bones whitening.

I slouched up hills of ice with polar bears,
practiced smell with the red fox,
trained my fangs with timber wolves.
I fight now for the rights to a carcass.
The killer who crouches, gets set, and leaps
is a kinsman I can call my cousin.
The strangling gibberish of the gorilla
comes out of my anxious mouth.
Among a thousand ring-tailed monkeys
scratching buttocks, sharing fleas,
shinning up trees in guatemala, I am one.
Among the blue-rumped baboons,
chattering chimpanzees and leering orangoutangs,
I am at home using paws for hands, hands for paws.
The howl of one hyena eating another is mine.
    In a boneless tube of ooze
    I soaked dumb days with sponges
    off the gulfcoast sea-bottom.
    Now I am the parrot
    who picks up palaver and repeats it.
    Now I am the river-hog, the hippopotamus
    and I am the little bird who lives in his ear
    and tells him when to get up and where to go.
    I took a long sweet time learning to talk
    and now I carry many half-words not yet made,
    hankering hoodoo words taking shape in mud:
    protoplasm, spermatozoa, phantasms, taboos.
    In the pour of a thrush morningsong,

in the lonesome cry of a loon at moonrise,
is the rush of more half-words:

All horns are one horn
and I am the sheep, the goat,
the yak, the buffalo, the prongbuck.

All shells are one shell
and I am the mussel clam,
the oyster, the mother-of-pearl.

I have been a freshwater polyp, a star-fish,
budding into evermore births of likeness
following likeness.

I have spent nights as kin of singing crickets,
meadow locusts, katydids, only the males singing,
the females silent and waiting.
I have been the calling frog with a bubble at his
throat—and the spotted snake who came to spell
doom and appeasement of hunger.

I have spoken as a brother to the walking stick
and the hesitations of his stilts and knee-joints.

I am the penguin and ostrich
trying to remember lost wings.
    I am the snake who had many legs
    trying to remember my lost legs.

        I have had a thousand fish faces, sea faces,
        sliding off into land faces, monkey faces—
            I began in a dim green mist
                                    of floating faces.

I have worn covers of thick strong hair and smooth fur.
I have shed rain and sleet with my feathers and down.
I have carried thick wool wrapping me warm as I slept in snow.
I have had tropic and arctic garments bestowed on me.

. . .

Since death is there in the light of the sun, in the song of the wind,
Since death is there in the marvel of the sun coming up to travel its
    arc and go down saying, "I am time and you are time,"
Since death is there in the slow creep of every dawn and in all the
    steps of shadow moving into evening and dusk of stars,
Since death is there in almost inaudible chimes of every slow clock-
    tick beginning at the birth hour there must be a tremor of music
    in the last little gong, the pling of the final announcement from
    the Black Void.

Have I not seen forms
flowing into faces and voices—
numbers hoarse and high with the mating cry
over rolling white sea-horses and forked lightning,
over the infinite velvet of blue land-fog,
over sacramental bread and heavy blood roses,
over mate-brown pigeons flying into burnt wilderness,
gazing into star-pool waters holding the great serene
                                        constellations?

I meditate with the mud eel
on where we came from.
Not yet can I give the scream speech
of a great white albatross—
frozen foam and sea-drift for her
high on an iceberg's shining white hat,
whirr and sweep of her wings
in the splinters of an arc of northern lights.

I am a three-hundred-year-old galapagos turtle,
sleeping and eating, eating and sleeping,
blinking and easy, sleepy-eyed and easy,
while shakespeare writes a flock of plays,
while john bunyan sits in jail and writes a book,
while cromwell, napoleon, lincoln, wilson, lenin,
      come and go, stride and vanish
while bryan, morgan, rockefeller, lafollette, altgeld,
      become names spelled and written.
I sleep, forget, remember, forget again, and ask:
      What of it?
      Don't bother me, brother.
      Don't bother a dozing turtle
      born to contemplate and yawn.

I was a scorpion and a tarantula
before the first huts of guadalajara,
before the first aztecs gathered bananas.
I was a maroon cockatoo and a green parakeet
before the first incas fashioned bird-cages.
In western nebraska I was a wild prairie pony
with a white forelock down my sorrel face
before ever a caesar or alexander or any czar
dreamed the smoke-shadow of a dream
of shattering armies beyond the horizon
                              and taking over.
What is this burden I carry out of yesterday?
Why am I so wise, so grand, so cunning, so ignorant?
What have I made that I haven't broken?
What have I bred that I haven't killed?
Why have I prized my skills as a killer?
What jargons, what gibberish, must I yet unlearn?
What are these bygones of dreams, moans, shadows?

Who are these people I come from who follow the ways
of long-gone time and long-gone fathers?

    What are these bygones
      sea-brought and land-locked?
For I am one and all of them:
they swarm in me with song, cry and murmur;
they fill my room with scurrying fish,
with apes and kangaroos, with swine and birds;
they bring arenas and theaters of action
wherein they kill, eat, crave, sing, live on,
or perish before the might of the stronger;
they stir with bleats and moans;
they fade with growls and chuckles.

They dream in me
and rise dripping on sea horizons
to shout hosannahs, to cry thanks,
to vanish leaving no sign nor track
on the silent lines of green mist.

    The earth rocked me
    in a cradle of winds.
    The fog and the mud
    clung as a wrap and home
    of swaddling cloths.
    And the sea sang bye-lo bye-lo
    and the stars and the rains
    brought changing songs: so-long so-long
    joined to the sea's old bye-lo bye-lo.
      . . .

Deep roots moving in lush soil to send a silver-gray beech tree
    straight toward the sky—

Shallow roots in barren land sending their stalks of grass and weeds
up over to bend in the wind with whisper tones—

Tangled and winding roots in desert wastes rising into cactus and
the joshua tree to bring a hush on the air with spare and mur-
muring blossoms wrought from dews of night air—

Am I, are you, kin to these everliving roots? Have you, have I, one
time long ago been an oak with a wind song in our leaves?

Have the bones of your torso spoken low to a sugar maple in october
flaming in branch and leaf: "We can not be strangers, I know
how you are what you are in root and trunk."

   . . .

I have said to the elephant and the flea, "Each of us makes his life in
what to him is the Known and for each of us there is a vast
Unknown and farther beyond the vaster Unknowable—and the
Ignorance we share and share alike is immeasurable."

The one-eyed mollusc on the sea-bottom, feathered and luminous,
is my equal in what he and I know of star clusters not yet found
by the best of star-gazers.

   . . .

The earth is a forgotten cinder.
A heaving fireball cooled off.
Thus the story of the rocks.
Each river came later than the cooling.
Next comes the freezing of the globe.
A heaving iceball will travel alone.
The rivers will be too cold to move.
Each flowering valley will be a memory.
The autobiography of a wild rose will run:
My leaves pressed between the times
           of a fireball and an iceball.

   . . .

I have been woven among meshes of long ropes
and fine filaments: older than the rocks and
fresh as the dawn of this morning today are
the everliving roots who begot me,
who poured me as one more seeker
one more swimmer in the gold and gray procession
of phantoms laughing, fighting, singing, moan-
ing toward the great cool calm of the fixed
return to the filaments of dust.

    I am more than a traveler out of Nowhere.
    Sea and land, sky and air, begot me Somewhere.
    Where I go from here and now, or if I go at all
      again, the Maker of sea and land, of sky and
      air, can tell.
      . . .

There is only one horse on the earth
and his name is All Horses.
There is only one bird in the air
and his name is All Wings.
There is only one fish in the sea
and his name is All Fins.
There is only one man in the world
and his name is All Men.
There is only one woman in the world
and her name is All Women.
There is only one child in the world
and the child's name is All Children.
    There is only one Maker in the world
    and His children cover the earth
    and they are named All God's Children.

MUSINGS

We have watched The Poet at his window, lounging deep in his chair, his powerful hands knotted, his dark, rugged face locked in a solemn dream. The poems, themselves, have been on exhibition at various stages. as pencilled yellow slips, as clean sheets retyped for the printer, as long rolls of galley-proofs.

——HENRY JUSTIN SMITH, from *Deadlines*

✿ *Chicago Poet*

I saluted a nobody.
I saw him in a looking-glass.
He smiled—so did I.
He crumpled the skin on his forehead,
    frowning—so did I.
Everything I did he did.
I said, "Hello, I know you."
And I was a liar to say so.

Ah, this looking-glass man!
Liar, fool, dreamer, play-actor,
Soldier, dusty drinker of dust—
Ah! he will go with me
Down the dark stairway
When nobody else is looking,
When everybody else is gone.

He locks his elbow in mine,
I lose all—but not him.

✿ *Phizzog*

This face you got,
This here phizzog you carry around,
You never picked it out for yourself,
    at all, at all—did you?

This here phizzog—somebody handed it
 to you—am I right?
Somebody said, "Here's yours, now go see
 what you can do with it."
Somebody slipped it to you and it was like
 a package marked:
"No goods exchanged after being taken away"—
This face you got.

❧ *Wilderness*

There is a wolf in me . . . fangs pointed for tearing gashes . . . a red
 tongue for raw meat . . . and the hot lapping of blood—I keep
 this wolf because the wilderness gave it to me and the wilderness
 will not let it go.

There is a fox in me . . . a silver-gray fox . . . I sniff and guess . . . I
 pick things out of the wind and air . . . I nose in the dark night
 and take sleepers and eat them and hide the feathers . . . I circle
 and loop and double-cross.

There is a hog in me . . . a snout and a belly . . . a machinery for
 eating and grunting . . . a machinery for sleeping satisfied in the
 sun—I got this too from the wilderness and the wilderness will
 not let it go.

There is a fish in me . . . I know I came from salt-blue water-
 gates . . . I scurried with shoals of herring . . . I blew waterspouts
 with porpoises . . . before land was . . . before the water went
 down . . . before Noah . . . before the first chapter of Genesis.

There is a baboon in me . . . clambering-clawed . . . dog-faced . . .
 yawping a galoot's hunger . . . hairy under the armpits . . . here

are the hawk-eyed hankering men . . . here are the blonde and blue-eyed women . . . here they hide curled asleep waiting . . . ready to snarl and kill . . . ready to sing and give milk . . . waiting—I keep the baboon because the wilderness says so.

There is an eagle in me and a mockingbird . . . and the eagle flies among the Rocky Mountains of my dreams and fights among the Sierra crags of what I want . . . and the mockingbird warbles in the early forenoon before the dew is gone, warbles in the under-brush of my Chattanoogas of hope, gushes over the blue Ozark foothills of my wishes—And I got the eagle and the mocking-bird from the wilderness.

O, I got a zoo, I got a menagerie, inside my ribs, under my bony head, under my red-valve heart—and I got something else: it is a man-child heart, a woman-child heart: it is a father and mother and lover: it came from God-Knows-Where: it is going to God-Knows-Where—For I am the keeper of the zoo: I say yes and no: I sing and kill and work: I am a pal of the world: I came from the wilderness.

🌺 Broken-Face Gargoyles

All I can give you is broken-face gargoyles.
It is too early to sing and dance at funerals,
Though I can whisper to you I am looking for an undertaker hum-ming a lullaby and throwing his feet in a swift and mystic buck-and-wing, now you see it and now you don't.

Fish to swim a pool in your garden flashing a speckled silver,
A basket of wine-saps filling your room with flame-dark for your eyes and the tang of valley orchards for your nose,

Such a beautiful pail of fish, such a beautiful peck of apples, I cannot bring you now.
It is too early and I am not footloose yet.

I shall come in the night when I come with a hammer and saw.
I shall come near your window, where you look out when your eyes open in the morning,
And there I shall slam together bird-houses and bird-baths for wing-loose wrens and hummers to live in, birds with yellow wing tips to blur and buzz soft all summer,
So I shall make little fool homes with doors, always open doors for all and each to run away when they want to.
I shall come just like that even though now it is early and I am not yet footloose,
Even though I am still looking for an undertaker with a raw, wind-bitten face and a dance in his feet.
I make a date with you (put it down) for six o'clock in the evening a thousand years from now.

All I can give you now is broken-face gargoyles.
All I can give you now is a double gorilla head with two fish mouths and four eagle eyes hooked on a street wall, spouting water and looking two ways to the ends of the street for the new people, the young strangers, coming, coming, always coming.

It is early.
I shall yet be footloose.

🌿 Aprons of Silence

Many things I might have said today.
And I kept my mouth shut.
So many times I was asked
To come and say the same things
Everybody was saying, no end

To the yes-yes, yes-yes,
      me-too, me-too.

The aprons of silence covered me.
A wire and hatch held my tongue.
I spit nails into an abyss and listened.
I shut off the gabble of Jones, Johnson, Smith,
All whose names take pages in the city directory.

I fixed up a padded cell and lugged it around.
I locked myself in and nobody knew it.
Only the keeper and the kept in the hoosegow
Knew it—on the streets, in the post office,
On the cars, into the railroad station
Where the caller was calling, "All a-board,
All a-board for . . . Blaa-blaa . . . Blaa-blaa,
Blaa-blaa . . . and all points northwest . . . all a-board."
Here I took along my own hoosegow
And did business with my own thoughts.
Do you see? It must be the aprons of silence.

🌺 The Road and the End

I shall foot it
Down the roadway in the dusk,
Where shapes of hunger wander
And the fugitives of pain go by.
I shall foot it
In the silence of the morning,
See the night slur into dawn,
Hear the slow great winds arise
Where tall trees flank the way
And shoulder toward the sky.

The broken boulders by the road
Shall not commemorate my ruin.
Regret shall be the gravel under foot.
I shall watch for
Slim birds swift of wing
That go where wind and ranks of thunder
Drive the wild processionals of rain.

The dust of the traveled road
Shall touch my hands and face.

🌺 Style

Style—go ahead talking about style.
You can tell where a man gets his style just
    as you can tell where Pavlowa got her legs
    or Ty Cobb his batting eye.

    Go on talking.
Only don't take my style away.
      It's my face.
      Maybe no good
          but anyway, my face.
I talk with it, I sing with it, I see, taste and feel with it, I know why
    I want to keep it.

Kill my style
             and you break Pavlowa's legs,
             and you blind Ty Cobb's batting eye.

🌺 Potato Blossom Songs and Jigs

    Rum tiddy um,
    tiddy um,
    tiddy um tum tum.
My knees are loose-like, my feet want to sling their selves.
I feel like tickling you under the chin—honey—and a-asking: Why
    Does a Chicken Cross the Road?

When the hens are a-laying eggs, and the roosters pluck-pluck-put-
    akut and you—honey—put new potatoes and gravy on the ta-
    ble, and there ain't too much rain or too little:
        Say, why do I feel so gabby?
        Why do I want to holler all over the place?

        . . .

Do you remember I held empty hands to you
    and I said all is yours
    the handfuls of nothing?

        . . .

I ask you for white blossoms.
I bring a concertina after sunset under the apple trees.
I bring out "The Spanish Cavalier" and "In the Gloaming, O My
    Darling."
The orchard here is near and home-like.
The oats in the valley run a mile.
Between are the green and marching potato vines.
The lightning bugs go criss-cross carrying a zigzag of fire: the potato
    bugs are asleep under their stiff and yellow-striped wings: here
    romance stutters to the western stars, "Excuse . . . me . . ."

        . . .

Old foundations of rotten wood.
An old barn done-for and out of the wormholes ten-legged roaches
    shook up and scared by sunlight.
So a pickax digs a long tooth with a short memory.
Fire can not eat this rubbish till it has lain in the sun.

        . . .

The story lags.
The story has no connections.
The story is nothing but a lot of banjo plinka planka plunks.

The roan horse is young and will learn: the roan horse buckles into
    harness and feels the foam on the collar at the end of a haul: the
    roan horse points four legs to the sky and rolls in the red clover:
    the roan horse has a rusty jag of hair between the ears hanging
    to a white star between the eyes.

.   .   .

In Burlington long ago
And later again in Ashtabula
I said to myself:
    I wonder how far Ophelia went with Hamlet.
What else was there Shakespeare never told?
There must have been something.
If I go bugs I want to do it like Ophelia.
There was class to the way she went out of her head.

.   .   .

Does a famous poet eat watermelon?
Excuse me, ask me something easy.
I have seen farmhands with their faces in fried catfish on a Monday
    morning.
And the Japanese, two-legged like us,
The Japanese bring slices of watermelon into pictures.
The black seeds make oval polka dots on the pink meat.

Why do I always think of niggers and buck-and-wing dancing
    whenever I see watermelon?

Summer mornings on the docks I walk among bushel peach baskets
    piled ten feet high.
Summer mornings I smell new wood and the river wind along with
    peaches.

I listen to the steamboat whistle hong-honging, hong-honging across
     the town.
And once I saw a teameo straddling a street with a hay-rack load of
     melons.

           . . .

Niggers play banjos because they want to.
The explanation is easy.

It is the same as why people pay fifty cents for tickets to a police-
     men's masquerade ball or a grocers-and-butchers' picnic with a
     fat man's foot race.
It is the same as why boys buy a nickel's worth of peanuts and eat
     them and then buy another nickel's worth.
Newsboys shooting craps in a back alley have a fugitive understand-
     ing of the scientific principle involved.
The jockey in a yellow satin shirt and scarlet boots, riding a sorrel
     pony at the county fair, has a grasp of the theory.
It is the same as why boys go running lickety-split
     away from a school-room geography lesson
     in April when the crawfishes come out
     and the young frogs are calling
     and the pussywillows and the cat-tails
     know something about geography themselves.

           . . .

I ask you for white blossoms.
I offer you memories and people.
I offer you a fire zigzag over the green and marching vines.
I bring a concertina after supper under the home-like apple trees.
I make up songs about things to look at:
     potato blossoms in summer night mist filling the garden with
        white spots;

a cavalryman's yellow silk handkerchief stuck in a flannel
   pocket over the left side of the shirt, over the ventricles of
   blood, over the pumps of the heart.

Bring a concertina after sunset under the apple trees.
Let romance stutter to the western stars, "Excuse . . . me . . ."

🌺 Cool Tombs

When Abraham Lincoln was shoveled into the tombs, he forgot the
   copperheads and the assassin . . . in the dust, in the cool tombs.

And Ulysses Grant lost all thought of con men and Wall Street, cash
   and collateral turned ashes . . . in the dust, in the cool tombs.

Pocahontas' body, lovely as a poplar, sweet as a red haw in Novem-
   ber or a pawpaw in May, did she wonder? does she remem-
   ber? . . . in the dust, in the cool tombs?

Take any streetful of people buying clothes and groceries, cheering
   a hero or throwing confetti and blowing tin horns . . . tell me if
   the lovers are losers . . . tell me if any get more than the
   lovers . . . in the dust . . . in the cool tombs.

🌺 Old Osawatomie

John Brown's body under the morning stars.
Six feet of dust under the morning stars.
And a panorama of war performs itself
Over the six-foot stage of circling armies.

Room for Gettysburg, Wilderness, Chickamauga,
On a six-foot stage of dust.

🐝 Hats

Hats, where do you belong?
    what is under you?

On the rim of a skyscraper's forehead
I looked down and saw: hats: fifty thousand hats:
Swarming with a noise of bees and sheep, cattle and waterfalls,
Stopping with a silence of sea grass, a silence of prairie corn.
    Hats: tell me your high hopes.

🐝 Accomplished Facts

Every year Emily Dickinson sent one friend
the first arbutus bud in her garden.

In a last will and testament Andrew Jackson
remembered a friend with the gift of George
Washington's pocket spy-glass.

Napoleon too, in a last testament, mentioned a silver
watch taken from the bedroom of Frederick the Great,
and passed along this trophy to a particular friend.

O. Henry took a blood carnation from his coat lapel
and handed it to a country girl starting work in a
bean bazaar, and scribbled: "Peach blossoms may or
may not stay pink in city dust."

So it goes. Some things we buy, some not.
Tom Jefferson was proud of his radishes, and Abe
Lincoln blacked his own boots, and Bismarck called
Berlin a wilderness of brick and newspapers.

So it goes. There are accomplished facts.
Ride, ride, ride on in the great new blimps—
Cross unheard-of oceans, circle the planet.
When you come back we may sit by five hollyhocks.
We might listen to boys fighting for marbles.
The grasshopper will look good to us.

So it goes . . .

Buffalo Dusk

The buffaloes are gone.
And those who saw the buffaloes are gone.
Those who saw the buffaloes by thousands and how they pawed the
    prairie sod into dust with their hoofs, their great heads down
    pawing on in a great pageant of dusk,
Those who saw the buffaloes are gone.
And the buffaloes are gone.

The Abracadabra Boys

The abracadabra boys—have they been in the stacks and cloisters?
    Have they picked up languages for throwing into chow mein
    poems?
Have they been to a sea of jargons and brought back jargons? Their
    salutations go: Who cometh? and, It ith I cometh.
They know postures from impostures, pistils from pustules, to hear
    them tell it. They foregather and make pitty pat with each other
    in Latin and in their private pig Latin, very ofay.
They give with passwords. "Who cometh?" "A kumquat cometh."
    "And how cometh the kumquat?" "On an abbadabba, ancient
    and honorable sire, ever and ever on an abbadabba."
Do they have fun? Sure—their fun is being what they are, like our
    fun is being what we are—only they are more sorry for us being
    what we are than we are for them being what they are.
Pointing at you, at us, at the rabble, they sigh and say, these abraca-
    dabra boys, "They lack jargons. They fail to distinguish between
    pustules and pistils. They knoweth not how the kumquat cometh."

Our Hells

Milton unlocked hell for us
and let us have a look.
Dante did the same.
Each of these hells is special.

One is Milton's, one Dante's.
Milton put in all that for him
    was hell on earth.
Dante put in all that for him
    was hell on earth.
If you unlock your hell for me
And I unlock my hell for you

They will be two special hells,
Each of us showing what for us
    is hell on earth.
Yours is one hell, mine another.

🐛 *Moonlight and Maggots*

The moonlight filters on the prairie.
The land takes back an old companion.
The young corn seems pleased with a visit.
In Illinois, in Iowa, this moontime is on.
A bongo looks out and talks about the look of the moon
As if always a bongo must talk somewhat so in moontime—
    The moon is a milk-white love promise,
    A present for the young corn to remember,
    A caress for silk-brown tassels to come.
    Spring moon to autumn moon measures one harvest.
    All almanacs are merely so many moon numbers.
    A house dizzy with decimal points and trick figures
    And a belfry at the top of the world for sleep songs
    And a home for lonesome goats to go to—
Like now, like always, the bongo takes up a moon theme—
There is no end to the ancient kit-kats inhabiting the moon:

Jack and the beanstalk and Jacob's ladder helped them up,
Cats and sheep, the albatross, the phoenix and the dodo-bird,
They are all living on the moon for the sake of the bongo—
Castles on the moon, mansions, shacks and shanties, ramshackle
Huts of tarpaper and tincans, grand real estate properties
Where magnificent rats eat tunnels in colossal cheeses,
Where the rainbow chasers take the seven prisms apart
And put them together again and are paid in moon money—
The flying dutchman, paul bunyan, saint paul, john bunyan,
The little jackass who coughs gold pieces when you say
    bricklebrit—
They are all there on the moon and the rent not paid
And the roof leaking and the taxes delinquent—
Like now, like always, the bongo jabbers of the moon,
Of cowsheds, railroad tracks, corn rows and cornfield corners
Finding the filter of the moon an old friend—
Look at it—cries the bongo—have a look! have a look!

    Well, what of it? comes the poohpooh—
Always the bongo is a little loony—comes the poohpooh,
The bongo is a poor fish and a long ways from home.
Be like me; be an egg, a hardboiled egg, a pachyderm
Practical as a buzzsaw and a hippopotamus put together.
Get the facts and no monkeybusiness what I mean.
The moon is a dead cinder, a ball of death, a globe of doom.
Long ago it died of lost motion, maggots masticated the surface
    of it
And the maggots languished, turned ice, froze on and took a free
    ride.
Now the sun shines on the maggots and the maggots make the
    moonlight.
The moon is a cadaver and a dusty mummy and a damned rotten
    investment.

The moon is a liability loaded up with frozen assets and worthless
   paper.
Only the lamb, the sucker, the come-on, the little lost boy, has time
   for the moon.

   Well—says the bongo—you got a good argument.
I am a little lost boy and a long ways from home.
I am a sap, a pathetic fish, a nitwit and a lot more and worse you
   couldn't think of.
Nevertheless and notwithstanding and letting all you say be granted
   and acknowledged
The moon is a silver silhouette and a singing stalactite.
The moon is a bringer of fool's gold and fine phantoms.
On the heaving restless sea or the fixed and fastened land
The moon is a friend for the lonesome to talk with.
The moon is at once easy and costly, cheap and priceless.
The price of the moon runs beyond all adding machine numbers
Summer moonmusic drops down adagio sostenuto whathaveyou.
Winter moonmusic practices the mind of man for a long trip.
The price of the moon is an orange and a few kind words.
Nobody on the moon says, I been thrown out of better places than
   this.
No one on the moon has ever died of arithmetic and hard words.
No one on the moon would skin a louse to sell the hide.
The moon is a pocket luckpiece for circus riders, for acrobats on the
   flying rings, for wild animal tamers.
I can look up at the moon and take it or leave it.
The moon coaxes me: Be at home wherever you are.
I can let the moon laugh me to sleep for nothing.
I can put a piece of the moon in my pocket for tomorrow.
I can holler my name at the moon and the moon hollers back my
   name.
When I get confidential with the moon and tell secrets

The moon is a sphinx and a repository under oath.

    Yes Mister poohpooh
I am a poor nut, just another of God's mistakes.
You are a tough bimbo, hard as nails, yeah.
You know enough to come in when it rains.
You know the way to the post office and I have to ask.
They might fool you the first time but never the second.
Thrown into the river you always come up with a fish.
You are a diller a dollar, I am a ten o'clock scholar.
You know the portent of the axiom: Them as has gits.
You devised that abracadabra: Get all you can keep all you get.

    We shall always be interfering with each other, forever be
    arguing—you for the maggots, me for the moon.
Over our bones, cleaned by the final maggots as we lie recumbent,
    perfectly forgetful, beautifully ignorant—
        There will settle over our grave illustrious tombs
        On nights when the air is clear as a bell
        And the dust and fog are shovelled off on the wind—
        There will sink over our empty epitaphs
                        a shiver of moonshafts
                        a line of moonslants.

🙣 *Biography*

A biography, sirs, should begin—with the breath of a man
when his eyes first meet the light of day—then working on
through to the death when the light of day is gone:
so the biography then is finished—unless you reverse the order
and begin with the death and work back to the birth—
starting the life with a coffin, moving back to a cradle—

in which case, sirs, the biography has arrived, is completed
when you have your subject born, except for ancestry, lineage,
forbears, pedigree, blood, breed, bones, backgrounds—
      and these, sirs, may be carried far.

🍃 *Breathing Tokens*

I

You must expect to be in several lost causes
  before you die.
Why blame your father and mother for your being
  born; how could they help what they were doing?
And their fathers and mothers farther back? Can we
  say they could help what they were doing?
Why rebuke old barns the wind has not yet blown away?
Why call down anathema on weather lacking ears to hear
  your opinion of it?
Are there historic moments when old Mother Justice, blind-
  folded so she can look and weigh without prejudice
Should make an entry and say with a low contralto of
  pause and finality, "Everybody is wrong and
               nobody is to blame?"

2

  There's no harm in trying.
  Nothing can harm you till it comes.
  And it may never come.
Or if it comes it is something else again.
And those who say, "I'll try anything once,"

often try nothing twice, three times,
arriving late at the gate of dreams worth dying for.

3

Be a leopard: set aside six minutes a day: count your spots.
   Try rubbing out the spots: see how it works.
   Write box car numbers on the white spots.
   Put sevens and elevens on the black spots.
   Say out loud, "I am a Numbah One Leopard—
"I was not born a two spot: hear me, heeyah me, I am Numbah
   One."
Of course, Mistah Man, this is out of your class.
You are not so silly as to sit counting your spots.
You would not be saying, "Heeyah me, I am Numbah One."
   Or be a giraffe and say:
"This neck is beyond question to identify me if I get lost"
Or: "My necklength is fixed by law and is therefore proper."
Yes be a giraffe: you got a right to try it.
Look down longnecked on those born shortnecked.
Chew the choice leaves of trees: tell others to eat grass.
Of course, Mistah Man, you draw elegant distinctions.

4

   Be a zebra: wear stripes
   Cultivate the sport model look.
Let others place their bets on whether you are
a white jackass with black stripes or vice versa.
   Wear anything you want to wear.
   Or wear what everybody is wearing.

Be the father of five alligators, five sharks.
Teach the little ones to take care of their teeth
and the value of teeth in earning a living.

Or be born, if you can, among the swift fish.
Learn how to go over and under, sidewise, zigzag.
Let the sliding of a snake on its belly be a lesson.
Study the elephant: he considers it an honor to eat hay
and to kill only when some killer comes to kill him.
He addresses the aggressor: "Why bother me? I warned you
                                    not to bother me."

Try being a goat: put on a face of calm contemplations.
Look people in the eye as though unaware they gaze at you.
    Read their innermost hidden secrets.
Then turn away toward other horizons chewing your cud.
How should their sins and prides be anything to you?
What have they learned of alfalfa and soy bean hay
or the somersaults of kids born for acrobatics?

                5

Be a bottle: say glug-glug: be a clock: say tick-tock.
Study why the clock never glugs
and why the bottle might try telling time and fail.
Consider the origins of men saying horsefeathers
                                    yes horsefeathers.

                6

Inquire into the monotony of shirts soiled
going to the laundry and returning to be soiled,
how each proud man is every so often sent to the cleaners,
how the bottle sellers rejoice over news of broken bottles.

Inquire further into the high contrasts
between those who can eat glass and like it
and connoisseurs who require bottled velvet,
and fixity of one living oceanic squid
and flights of those who are born birds.
Shall the squid have praise or blame for being a squid?
Shall the bird have compliments for being born with wings?
   What shall a broken bottle
   tell a brand new bottle?
   "Your time will come—
        you'll get yours"
        something like that?

                    7

Be what you want to be.
An oak, a blossom, a dry leaf in the wind
or the wind blowing the dry leaf; or both.
Be a gong or three gongs in one: a gong of silence:
A gong of clamor crying hellsbells to the satisfied:
A gong of smooth songs saying yes and welcome.
Be what an earthworm means to be
in the measure of its circumference
so humble so slow so true
to the date of the stars it was born under.

Your personal doorways know your shadows
and number the times you enter, exit, enter
so often having no lines to say
though you are actor and audience to yourself.

Thrust laughter from your diaphragm whensoever.
Be perpendicular till the finish.
You will be horizontal long enough afterward

with toes shoving up the daisies
yielding to the earth's ancient mulch.

8

Be ice: be fire.
Be hard and take the smoothing of brass for your own.
Be sensitized with winter quicksilver below zero.
Be tongs and handles: find breathing tokens.
See where several good dreams are worth dying for.

❧ Monday, One P.M.

Fix it up like an affidavit with a notary's seal: Sworn to before me
    this day—'twon't do any good in this case—either you get it or
    you don't.

I dropped into the I.W.W. headquarters and talked with Bill Hay-
    wood and Russ, Italian and Slovak organizers handling a strike
    at Pullman
And Haywood was wondering how in hell Robert T. Lincoln, chair-
    man of the board of directors of the Pullman Company, ever
    sprang from the loins of Abraham Lincoln, the finest guy of all
    of 'em in American history
And the Russ organizer said the Pullman officers were a lot of liars
    telling the newspapers a ten per cent pay raise was going to all
    the Pullman workers
And the Slovak swore and said women were going crazy out at
    Pullman trying to raise families and keep their boys and girls
    straight on nineteen cents an hour for yard-men and roustabouts.

Well, I picked up a telephone to call Amy Lowell at the Congress
Hotel and tell her what a good job she did writing about the life
of Emile Verhaeren, the Belgian working-class poet.
It was a party line and two men were talking. One said: May Blos-
som is the greatest bitch in the world; she's only six months old
but you can count on it she's the greatest bitch the world has ever
seen.
How does she behave?—came the query; and the answer was: You
never saw a bulldog bitch in your life more gentle; I raised her
myself; I would trust my mother with her.
And the talk ran on litters and whelps, brindles and fawns, ending
with the price of May Blossom, rated as the world's greatest
bitch, fixed at one hundred seventy-five dollars.

And when they hung up I got Amy at the Congress. I told her I was
sorry I missed her lecture on Imagism the night before at the
Little Theatre and I'd like to come over and ask her some ques-
tions about Emile Verhaeren, the Belgian working-class poet.
Amy said she just finished breakfast one o'clock in the afternoon,
she reads all night instead of sleeping, and she'd try to arrange
her program so I'd get a look-in.
I told her I felt kind of restless about the new poetry and I had high
hopes the new poetry one way or another would be able to get
at the real stuff of American life, slipping its fingers into the steel
meshes and copper coils of it under the streets and over the
houses and people and factories and groceries, conceding a fair
batting average to Dante and Keats for what they wrote about
love and roses and the moon.

❧ Government

The Government—I heard about the Government and I went out to find it. I said I would look closely at it when I saw it.

Then I saw a policeman dragging a drunken man to the calaboose. It was the Government in action.

I saw a ward alderman slip into an office one morning and talk with a judge. Later in the day the judge dismissed a case against a pickpocket who was a live ward worker for the alderman. Again I saw this was the Government, doing things.

I saw militiamen level their rifles at a crowd of workingmen who were trying to get other workingmen to stay away from a shop where there was a strike on. Government in action.

Everywhere I saw that Government is a thing made of men, that Government has blood and bones, it is many mouths whispering into many ears, sending telegrams, aiming rifles, writing orders, saying "yes" and "no."

Government dies as the men who form it die and are laid away in their graves and the new Government that comes after is human, made of heartbeats of blood, ambitions, lusts, and money running through it all, money paid and money taken, and money covered up and spoken of with hushed voices.

A Government is just as secret and mysterious and sensitive as any human sinner carrying a load of germs, traditions and corpuscles handed down from fathers and mothers away back.

I Should Like to Be Hanged on a Summer Afternoon

I have often thought I should like to be hanged
On a summer afternoon in daylight, the sun shining and bands
   playing,
In a park or on a public square or a main street corner,
   everybody in town looking on and talking about it,
Newspaper extras spelling my name in tall headlines telling the
   town I am getting hanged.

And I smile to the sheriff and say he will be laughed at if the
   rope breaks
And he goes puttering, solemn, doing a duty under the law,
Feeling the ropes, searching corners, testing scantlings.

And before the cap is drawn over my head
And before my feet are tied for the straight drop,
When I am asked if I have any last word to say before I go to
   meet my God and Maker;
I speak in a cool, even voice, fixing my eyes maybe on some
   dark-eyed mother in the crowd, a grown dark-eyed daughter
   leaning against her.
I speak and say, "I am innocent and I am ready to meet my
   God face to face" . . .

I have often thought I should like to be hanged that way on a
   summer afternoon in daylight, the sun shining and bands
   playing.

❧ POETRY DEFINITIONS

Poetry is the achievement of the synthesis of hyacinths and biscuits.

— CARL SANDBURG, No. 36 from "Tentative (First Model) Definitions of Poetry," in *Good Morning, America*

✿ Tentative (First Model) Definitions of Poetry

1   Poetry is a projection across silence of cadences arranged to break that silence with definite intentions of echoes, syllables, wave lengths.

2   Poetry is an art practised with the terribly plastic material of human language.

3   Poetry is the report of a nuance between two moments, when people say, 'Listen!' and 'Did you see it?' 'Did you hear it? What was it?'

4   Poetry is the tracing of the trajectories of a finite sound to the infinite points of its echoes.

5   Poetry is a sequence of dots and dashes, spelling depths, crypts, crosslights, and moon wisps.

6   Poetry is a puppet-show, where riders of skyrockets and divers of sea fathoms gossip about the sixth sense and the fourth dimension.

7   Poetry is a plan for a slit in the face of a bronze fountain goat and the path of fresh drinking water.

8   Poetry is a slipknot tightened around a time-beat of one thought, two thoughts, and a last interweaving thought there is not yet a number for.

9   Poetry is an echo asking a shadow dancer to be a partner.

10   Poetry is the journal of a sea animal living on land, wanting to fly the air.

11   Poetry is a series of explanations of life, fading off into horizons too swift for explanations.

12 Poetry is a fossil rock-print of a fin and a wing, with an illegible oath between.

13 Poetry is an exhibit of one pendulum connecting with other and unseen pendulums inside and outside the one seen.

14 Poetry is a sky dark with a wild-duck migration.

15 Poetry is a search for syllables to shoot at the barriers of the unknown and the unknowable.

16 Poetry is any page from a sketchbook of outlines of a doorknob with thumb-prints of dust, blood, dreams.

17 Poetry is a type-font design for an alphabet of fun, hate, love, death.

18 Poetry is the cipher key to the five mystic wishes packed in a hollow silver bullet fed to a flying fish.

19 Poetry is a theorem of a yellow-silk handkerchief knotted with riddles, sealed in a balloon tied to the tail of a kite flying in a white wind against a blue sky in spring.

20 Poetry is a dance music measuring buck-and-wing follies along with the gravest and stateliest dead-marches.

21 Poetry is a sliver of the moon lost in the belly of a golden frog.

22 Poetry is a mock of a cry at finding a million dollars and a mock of a laugh at losing it.

23 Poetry is the silence and speech between a wet struggling root of a flower and a sunlit blossom of that flower.

24 Poetry is the harnessing of the paradox of earth cradling life and then entombing it.

25 Poetry is the opening and closing of a door, leaving those who look through to guess about what is seen during a moment.

26 Poetry is a fresh morning spider-web telling a story of moonlit hours of weaving and waiting during a night.

27 Poetry is a statement of a series of equations, with numbers and symbols changing like the changes of mirrors, pools, skies, the only never-changing sign being the sign of infinity.

28 Poetry is a packsack of invisible keepsakes.

29 Poetry is a section of river-fog and moving boat-lights, delivered between bridges and whistles, so one says, 'Oh!' and another, 'How?'

30 Poetry is a kinetic arrangement of static syllables.

31 Poetry is the arithmetic of the easiest way and the primrose path, matched up with foam-flanked horses, bloody knuckles, and bones, on the hard ways to the stars.

32 Poetry is a shuffling of boxes of illusions buckled with a strap of facts.

33 Poetry is an enumeration of birds, bees, babies, butterflies, bugs, bambinos, babayagas, and bipeds, beating their way up bewildering bastions.

34 Poetry is a phantom script telling how rainbows are made and why they go away.

35 Poetry is the establishment of a metaphorical link between white butterfly-wings and the scraps of torn-up love-letters.

36 Poetry is the achievement of the synthesis of hyacinths and biscuits.

37 Poetry is a mystic, sensuous mathematics of fire, smoke-stacks, waffles, pansies, people, and purple sunsets.

38 Poetry is the capture of a picture, a song, or a flair, in a deliberate prism of words.

Acknowledgments

For permissions to publish, we are indebted to the Carl Sandburg Family Trust, Maurice C. Greenbaum and Philip G. Carson, Trustees, and to Robert Wedgeworth, University Librarian, University of Illinois at Urbana-Champaign. We are also indebted to Vicki Austin-Smith, Ruth Greenstein, and Sarah Longstaff for their continued help.

Original Publication Sources

All of the poems collected here, excluding the three previously unpublished Lincoln poems, originally appeared in the following volumes (books and poems listed in alphabetical order):

Billy Sunday and Other Poems, copyright © 1993 by Maurice C. Greenbaum and Frank M. Parker as Trustees of the Carl Sandburg Family Trust. Compilation, Introduction, and Notes copyright © 1993 by George Hendrick and Willene Hendrick: "Arms," "Billy Sunday," "Black Prophetess," "Cleo," "The *Eastland,*" "Eugene V. Debs," "Ezra," "Hawthorne," "Hellcat," "I Should Like to Be Hanged on a Summer Afternoon," "In Blue Gown and in Black Satin Gown," "An Interwoven Man and Woman Talked," "Jerry," "Legal Midnight Hour," "Man, the Man-Hunter," "Monday, One P.M.," "Napoleon," "Painted Fishes," "Planked Whitefish," "A Reporter in Debt," "She Held Herself a Deep Pool for Him," "Sherwood Anderson," "Taking on Suds Men Talk," "These Valleys Seem Old," "Troth Tryst," and "The Workingmen."

Breathing Tokens, copyright © 1978 by Maurice C. Greenbaum and Frank M. Parker, Trustees of the Sandburg Family Trust: "Breathing Tokens," "Bumble Bee Days," "Chinese Letters or Korean," "Evidence As to a She Devil," "From an Illinois Prairie Hut," "Good Babies Make Good Poems," "Journey and Oath," "Mr. Blake's Chariots," "Mr. Lincoln and His Gloves," "Nearer Than Any Mother's Heart Wishes," "Sojourner Truth Speaking," "To a Poet," and "You and a Sickle Moon."

The People, Yes, copyright 1936 by Harcourt Brace and Company. Copyright renewed 1964 by Carl Sandburg: "The People, Yes, Nos. 1, 4, 20, 37, 55, 57, 58, 78, 81, and 107."

Slabs of the Sunburnt West, copyright 1922 by Harcourt Brace and Company. Copyright renewed 1950 by Carl Sandburg: "Gypsy Mother," "Slabs of the Sunburnt West," "The Windy City," and "Without the Cane and the Derby."

Smoke and Steel, copyright 1920 by Harcourt Brace and Company. Copyright renewed 1948 by Carl Sandburg: "Accomplished Facts," "Aprons of Silence," "Baby Toes," "Broken-Face Gargoyles," "Buffalo Dusk," "Dan," "Glimmer," "Grieg Being Dead," "Hats," "Helga," "Hoodlums," "In the Shadow of the Palace," "Jack London and O. Henry," "Jazz Fantasia," "The Lawyers Know Too Much," "The Liars," "The Mayor of Gary," "My People," "Osawatomie," "Paula," "Red-Headed Restaurant Cashier," "Smoke and Steel," "Spanish," and "Threes."

Wind Song, copyright 1958, 1960 by Carl Sandburg. Copyright 1936 by Curtis Publishing Company. Copyright renewed 1986 by Margaret Sandburg, Helga Sandburg Crile, and Janet Sandburg: "Bee Song" and "Lines Written for Gene Kelly to Dance To."

The World of Carl Sandburg, copyright © 1961 by Carl Sandburg. Narration, Introduction, and Notes copyright © 1961 by Norman Corwin: "Elizabeth Umpstead" and "The Machine."

Selected Bibliography

Corwin, Norman. *The World of Carl Sandburg*. New York: Harcourt Brace & World, 1961.

Crowder, Richard. *Carl Sandburg*. New York: Twayne, 1964.

Golden, Harry. *Carl Sandburg*. Urbana, Ill.: University of Illinois Press, 1988.

Haas, Joseph and Gene Lovitz. *Carl Sandburg: A Pictorial Biography*. New York: Putnam, 1967.

Niven, Penelope. *Carl Sandburg: A Biography*. Urbana, Ill.: University of Illinois Press, 1994.

Sandburg, Carl. *Abraham Lincoln: The Prairie Years and The War Years*. New York: Harcourt, Brace, & World, 1954.

————. *Always the Young Strangers*. New York: Harcourt Brace, 1953.

————. *Billy Sunday and Other Poems*. Edited by George and Willene Hendrick. New York: Harcourt Brace & Company, 1993.

————. *Breathing Tokens*. Edited by Margaret Sandburg. New York: Harcourt Brace Jovanovich, 1978.

————. *Chicago Poems*. New York: Henry Holt, 1916.

————. *The Complete Poems of Carl Sandburg*, revised and expanded edition. New York: Harcourt Brace Jovanovich, 1970.

————. *Cornhuskers*. New York: Henry Holt, 1918.

————. *Good Morning, America*. New York: Harcourt Brace, 1928.

————. *Harvest Poems, 1910–1960*. New York: Harcourt Brace, 1960.

————. *Honey and Salt*. New York: Harcourt Brace & World, 1963.

————. *The People, Yes.* New York: Harcourt Brace, 1990.

————. *A Sandburg Treasury: Poetry and Prose for Young People.* New York: Harcourt Brace, 1970.

————. *Slabs of the Sunburnt West.* New York: Harcourt Brace, 1922.

————. *Smoke and Steel.* New York: Harcourt Brace and Howe, 1920.

————. *Wind Song.* New York: Harcourt Brace, 1960.

Sandburg, Margaret, ed. *The Poet and the Dream Girl: The Love Letters of Lilian Steichen and Carl Sandburg.* Urbana: University of Illinois Press, 1987.

Index of Titles and First Lines

About the Editors

George Hendrick is Professor of English at the University of Illinois at Urbana-Champaign. His publications include *Henry Salt: Humanitarian Reformer and Man of Letters; Remembrances of Concord and the Thoreaus; Toward the Making of Thoreau's Modern Reputation* (with Fritz Oehlschlaeger); *Thoreau Amongst Friends and Philistines, and Other Thoreauviana; Ever the Winds of Chance* (with Margaret Sandburg); *Fables, Foibles, and Foobles;* and *To Reach Eternity: The Letters of James Jones.*

Willene Hendrick is an independent scholar who lives in Urbana, Illinois. With George Hendrick she has published *On the Illinois Frontier: Dr. Hiram Rutherford, 1840–1848; Katherine Anne Porter,* revised edition; *The Savour of Salt: A Henry Salt Anthology; Ham Jones, Antebellum Southern Humorist: An Anthology;* and *Billy Sunday and Other Poems,* a collection of previously unpublished, uncollected, and unexpurgated works of Carl Sandburg.

Other books by Carl Sandburg available from Harcourt Brace & Company in Harvest paperback editions:

Abraham Lincoln: The Prairie Years and The War Years
Always the Young Strangers
The American Songbag
Billy Sunday and Other Poems
Harvest Poems
Honey and Salt
The People, Yes
Remembrance Rock

$15.00 Canada $21.00   Poetry

"WHAT Sandburg knew and said was what America knew from the beginning and said from the beginning and has not yet, no matter what is believed of her, forgotten how to say," wrote Archibald MacLeish about Carl Sandburg—that most American of poets—and his connection to the American psyche.

This new collection of Sandburg's poetry, which includes four previously unpublished Lincoln poems, contains selections from all of Sandburg's previous volumes and certainly supports MacLeish's confidence in the breadth of Sandburg's scope. In more than 150 poems, arranged in eleven sections—from Chicago to Poems of Protest to Lincoln to Anti-War Poems to Poet of the People—readers can see what Sandburg was made of and, in turn, what the poet thought the American people were made of. Sandburg's aim was to write "simple poems . . . which continue to have an appeal for simple people," and throughout his life the poet strove to maintain that important connection. The Hendricks, in a thoughtful and comprehensive introduction, discuss how Sandburg's life and beliefs colored his work and why that work resonates with Americans today.

Carl Sandburg (1878–1967) was born in Galesburg, Illinois, and worked a variety of jobs in renegade fashion. With the publication of Chicago Poems in 1915, however, he embarked on a literary career that brought him international fame as a poet, novelist, biographer, historian, journalist, and musician. George and Willene Hendrick, the editors of this volume, are closely associated with the Sandburg estate and the Sandburg collection at the University of Illinois. They live in Urbana, Illinois.

Edited by George and Willene Hendrick

Cover photograph by Dana Steichen
reprinted with permission of Joanna T. Steichen

Cover design by Scott Piehl

ISBN 0-15-600396-1

A Harvest Original
Harcourt Brace & Company
525 B Street, San Diego, CA 92101
15 East 26th Street, New York, NY 10010

9 780156 003964   90000>